PROFESSIONAL ACCOUNTABILITY
FOR
SOCIAL WORK PRACTICE

A Search for Concepts and Guidelines

EDITED BY

HELEN REHR

PRODIST
New York • 1979

PRODIST
a division of
Neale Watson Academic Publications, Inc.
156 Fifth Avenue
New York, New York 10010

© Neale Watson Academic Publications, Inc. 1979

Designed and manufactured in the U.S.A

Library of Congress Cataloging in Publication Data

Main entry under title:

Professional accountability for social work
    practice.

    Bibliography: p.
    1. Social service—United States—Evaluation—
Addresses, essays, lectures. I. Rehr, Helen.
HV91.P743   361   79–18691
ISBN 0–88202–127–3

Contents

Acknowledgements

This volume is the result of work by the staff of a Department of Social Work Services, entered upon in a spirit of search for self-directedness. The path was not without obstacles. All the social workers may well have felt imposed on and harassed for different purposes at different times, yet it was they who reflected on the problems, identified the obstacles, overcame their natural resistances, and persevered. In the end, those staff members demonstrated that their exploration reached the highest level of professional accountability—setting standards, assessing practice, analyzing, interpreting findings, and seeking continuing education for change.

Those of us who have written about these experiences did so in the belief that the learning process and its feedback loop bring about professional independence through the continuing search for new knowledge and its application. On the sidelines, always encouraging and supportive, was Mrs. Robert M. Benjamin, trusted friend of social work, who made available the resources of the Benjamin Educational Fund in order that this search might become a reality. To Marjorie Pleshette goes our indebtedness. She monitored the production of the volume, seeing to it that each of us got what we needed to complete our respective sections and was helpful at all times.

All of us welcome you to a professional adventure.

Preface

Professional accountability in the decade of the 1970s has assumed the proportions of a national fad, the latest indoor sport for the ethical, the obsessed, and the capricious. Accountability of all professions, both for authentic and false motivations, has come under increased surveillance and attack, with a parallel surge of research and standard-setting.

Although the presenting symptoms appear to arise from concerns with fraud, abuse, and error, it should be evident that more fundamental changes in society—social problems en masse, proliferation of technology, bureaucratization, value shifts—account for the multidimensional concerns with professional accountability. Professional practitioners have indulged their own self-doubts and concerns for the service systems to the point of masochism. Consumers, consumer advocates, administrators, the media, the man in the street, and, certainly government representatives feel compelled to rush forward with their own circumscribed solutions.

Nevertheless, it is important to recognize that each vocation or discipline that moves toward professional status does so by accepting a greater degree of accountability to the community that sanctions it. This is reflected in the legal regulation, the provision of resources, and the social institutions and customs that control professional behavior. With these societal shifts of values, praxis, and structures, other modes of accountability must be added.

In regard to social work practice, some deny the existence of accountability in order to elevate their own dogma; others attack it as a political diversion in order to reduce or alter services to people. Yet within that bedrock of daily social work practice, as this volume reveals, genuine responsibility and concern is alive and well.

The social work profession, by origin and mission, has a certain built-in accountability. Jane Addams, Mary Richmond,

Bertha Reynolds, Harriett Bartlett, their colleagues and successors, established a profession directed toward social accountability—to help meet the social and individual needs arising from the interactions of people and their social institutions. This accountability formed an essential ingredient in the disciplined, controlled use of oneself and in the recognition of the core of self-determination in each human being. It was nurtured in the apprenticeship nature of social work education, in the constant refinement of the supervision and consultation processes, in the social controls of the practice settings and the standards of the professional association.

Since Richard C. Cabot, M.D., in 1915 recognized social work as a profession distinct from its "poor but honest parents," "philanthropy" and "charity," social workers in health care settings have been in the vanguard of social work accountability.[1] The 1920s and 1930s were a period of many studies of social work practice and the social component in illness and medical care. As Bartlett[2] has described, the increasing influence of the psychiatric approach shifted the emphasis to the meaning of illness to the patient and family with greater focus on process. These practice experiences intermittently moved into the schools of social work and the continuing education programs of the professional association, creating high degrees of specialization. Such improvements in the precision of knowledge and practice constitute a basic part of professional accountability.

The search for the generic in social work of the 1950s and 1960s led to wide use of the concept of *social functioning* and encompassed the psyche, the soma, and the social. Such a broad conception introduced a more extensive view of the social worker's role and responsibility in the expanding health care system. Despite considerable disruption through challenges to social institutions in the last half of the 1960s, those challenges strengthened the *social functioning* concept by emphasizing professional accountability for system change and quality assurance.

In this decade, accountability by the social work profession has taken several forms. In the area of advancement of knowledge and practice, it has resulted in a resurgence of efforts by the National Association of Social Workers (NASW) to clarify the conceptual bases of practice[3] and the definition of specialization,[4] recently developed by the NASW/CSWE* Joint Task Force on Specialization. The growth of continuing education offerings by schools, agencies, NASW, and affinity groups, such as the Society of Hospital Social Service Directors, constitutes another response to accountability demand, mostly from practitioners themselves.

This activity has increased to the point where a joint task force of the National Association of Social Workers and the Council on Social Work Education is working on a baseline document of definition and responsibilities for the accountability effort. The historical weakness of practice-education interaction is being overcome by these joint issue-oriented task forces, and by the NASW policy drive to increase practice-education accountability through such techniques as including practitioners on school accreditation site-visit teams.

It is most important also to recognize the impact of expanded publication by NASW and by commercial publishers entering the field.

The functional area of standards development and enforcement has become the primary location of accountability efforts. Design of a six-level differential classification of the social work labor force and its promulgation in the field helped clarify the levels of professional accountability.[5] This differential classification standard has been translated into a three-level model statute for legal regulation, to establish minimum standards of practice. Twenty-four states now have legal regulation.

Quality assurance is being extended through objective examinations at the baccalaureate, master, and specialization stratum, building on the seven years of experience with the advance practice ACSW examination.

An aggressive program of standards development and enforcement has occurred, with these results:

1. Active adjudication of grievances for unethical practice
2. Printing and dissemination of a Register of Clinical Social Workers to promote standards and accountability
3. Revision of the standards of social work services departments in hospitals with a zealous drive for implementa-

*Council on Social Work Education, the accrediting body for schools of social work.

tion by the Joint Commission on Accreditation of Hospitals (JCAH)

4. Official entry and recognition of the social work profession on Accreditation Councils of the Joint Commission on Accreditation of Hospitals

5. Promotion of service standards through professional recognition, by government, insurance companies, and agencies, of vendorship status for social workers

A third major area of professional action directed toward improving the quality of practice centers on the legislative and judicial arenas. Long-term consultation and pressure by NASW introduced the social component of health care into Health Maintenance Organization (HMO) legislation by establishing required standards for social workers. The participation of social workers in the Professional Standards Review Organization (PSRO) mechanism was obtained in the same way, as was the End Stage Renal Disease Standards Review structure.

Direct intervention with the U.S. Civil Service Commission has obtained recognition/definition of social workers as providers in the Federal Employees Health Benefits Plan, the single largest health care program in the U.S.

All these methods for producing or strengthening accountability reflect the multidimensional nature of today's service systems. They draw on the expertise of the social work profession, tested in settings and schools through professional exchange and research. Valuable advances in knowledge are gained through examination and comparison of a variety of operations, as in the Coulton study of existing social work quality assurance programs in health care.[6]

However, the profession must ultimately depend upon the recording of the practice process and conceptualization that is so distinctive in this book. The transactions of highly motivated professionals, working in a facility with the reputation for quality service such as The Mount Sinai Hospital, offer a special opportunity to provide the profession with new perspectives as well as higher goals. The description of the various elements constituting a quality assurance program is a singular contribution to knowledge and practice, and to the people it serves. As Shakespeare wrote, "Come, give us a taste of your quality." Rehr and Company have given us a feast.

CHAUNCEY A. ALEXANDER, ACSW, CAE
Executive Director
National Association of Social Workers

References

1. Richard C. Cabot, M.D., *Social Service & The Art of Healing*, Boston, Moffat, Yard & Company, 1915. Reprinted, the NASW Classics Series, 1973. Washington, D.C., National Association of Social Workers, 1973, p. 39.

2. Harriett M. Bartlett, *Social Work Practice In The Health Field*, Washington, D.C., National Association of Social Workers, 1961, pp. 134–135.

3. See *Social Work*, "Special Issue on Conceptual Frameworks," Vol. 22, No. 5, September 1977, 444 pages.

4. "Specialization In The Social Work Profession," Washington, D.C., National Association of Social Work, November 1978. Multilithed.

5. *Standards for Social Service Manpower*, Washington, D.C., National Association of Social Workers, 1973, 19 pages.

6. Claudia J. Coulton, *Social Work Quality Assurance Programs—A Comparative Analysis*, Washington, D.C., National Association of Social Workers, 1978.

1

An Introduction to an Adventure in Professional Accountability

HELEN REHR

For the consumer seeking professional help, the questions are: "Will it help? Will it be good quality? Will it be caring?" For the reimbursing and regulatory agencies, the queries are: "Is it good quality? Is it effective? Is it reasonably priced?" Providers, professional and institutional, ask: "What are we responsible for? What is needed? How do we provide it? Is it beneficial and cost-effective?" The profession itself, which carries the responsibility for the quality of services delivered, asks: "Are we asking these questions of ourselves and seeking out the answers?"

The current concern with professional responsibility and accountability is symptomatic of broader concerns with inequities, misuse, fraud, and abuse, in general. The growing interest is the result of the breakdown in values and ethical behavior, particularly within the human services professions, and the failure of professions to be concerned with the "public good." The result is a two-way dilemma: growing suspicion, doubts, and demands on the part of the public and a rising wall of self-protection by the providers.

In viewing the health care system of today, it is possible to study the social work services in that system and note how closely they simulate the medical model in which they practice. The criticisms of fragmentation, inequity, limited accessibility and availability, and questionable quality plus ever-rising cost, which are ascribed to the medical care system, can be said of the social work system, as well. In spite of awareness of the failings in the medical care system, social work in health settings, makes excuses, mollifying patients and placating them for the deficits, while attempting to offer its own umbrella of "caring" that is so frequently absent elsewhere. Despite its denials, social work has remained the handmaiden of medicine, and of the hospitals in which it is practiced.

One of the hallmarks of a profession is that it sets standards by which its members are to practice, and has some means of designating those "who are able to meet the norms."[1] Such designation leads to the difference that distinguishes members of the profession from others. The standards assumed to be based on knowledge, skills, and qualities for social service are set to protect the public. "The primary goal of social work education is to prepare capable practitioners."[2] Qualified or competency-based education for practice is lodged in (1) "necessary, desirable, visible and effective service," (2) "effective practice behaviors—for specific purposes and yet flexibly utilizable in a number of settings," and (3) "assessment must be made through direct evaluation. . . ."[3] Yet when we look to the codes of ethics of such professions as medicine, law, and social work, we see that each concentrates on the *precise* characteristics needed to prepare a qualified professional in the field. In social work, the issue of competence was addressed by a listing of characteristics to meet standards for self-regulated practice. These included "professional autonomy," "integrated personal, social and professional values," "a broad knowledge of the range of social work concepts, methods and professional issues," "a depth of knowledge and technical skills in a specified method or combination of methods in a specific field of practice."[4]

In social work it has been generally assumed that necessary knowledge and personal attributes merge to create a qualified practitioner—an act of faith rather than empiricism. The NASW *Guidelines* conclude that the descriptive listing is "only a guide" and that the profession must await the development of "concrete and specific operational measures of assessment".[5] The committee assigned to the task of seeking "measures" of services rendered did what medicine, law, and the other professions do: it resolved them by identifying elements of the "curriculum vitae," including experience and publications, "reference vouchers" by others of the same status, "standardized tests" with "objective" questions, a "specimen of practice," and an "oral examination," given by peers—a most important beginning and, in a way, a milestone for a profession. The profession of social work has only recently begun the development of quality standards. Lewis says the "marketplace pressures" for standard setting are in constant operation by agencies, institutions, and government regulations. His concern is that they are provider- or institution-oriented, with little or no indication of consumer involvement; the client or the patient has not yet found a place in determination of quality. Pragmatism, frequently resulting from default of standards, becomes, Lewis believes, the self-serving means for standard-setting.[6]

Eveline Burns registers her concern with the lack of social work's professional accountability by citing its self-interest over the last few years in such issues as vendorship, reimbursement, fee-for-service.[7] Many would say these are survival concerns. Others contend that these are self-serving and not in the public good. The professional issue of "social contract" is at stake; in return for professional self-regulation, admission rites, and privileges, the public expects that the profession will safeguard the public trust and the public good.[8] Burns claims that it is difficult to consider quality of care in the public good, when the functional determinants of the profession are not clear. She poses the question, "What does social work do?" When the profession can define what it does, then quality of practice can be addressed.[9]

Fizdale further compounds the issue. She asks whether social work is truly a profession. Its failure to assume responsibility and accountability is lodged in the structures within which it practices. She suggests the educational demands placed on social work students indicate they may be trained as technicians, not professionals. "The difference has been sharpened between the accountability of a practitioner with "employee" status and that of an acknowledged professional. The former is hired to carry out assigned tasks within the limits of the employer's policies and procedures".[10] She notes that a responsible employee keeps his employer informed of the facts; there his accountability ends. The employer then decides what to do with the information. The employee may be dissatisfied with what is done or he may take "pride in the fact that he has contributed toward the improvement of the program."[11] But, as an employee, he can only be *indirectly* accountable to his client, by utilizing his influence and his ability to educate and persuade his employer. By contrast, the professional practitioner is primarily accountable to his clients, current and potential. He cannot avoid his responsibility for the quality of service he offers, whether given on his own as in private practice, or in conjunction with others as in a social agency,[12] or in a hospital. This means that professionals employed in service agencies and the administrators of those settings have a responsibility to work out in their relationships the professional implications in roles, responsibilities, and accountability.

The Mount Sinai Department of Social Work Services attempted to develop such a relationship; it entered upon an adventure. Many years ago it had begun to open up the complex area of professional accountability by trying to define its function, seeking to describe what social work does so that it could judge the outcome of its services. Berkman and Rehr, in their early study of utilization patterns of the elderly, involved the staff in an assessment of how and when cases entered the social work system. Their findings showed that social workers were dependent on referrals by others. This dependency meant that clients reached the social service system very late in their hospitalization.[13] These first attempts at audits resulted in the development of a social problem classification,[14] with the hope of giving definition to the human problems most frequently presented. They then moved on, attempting to codify resolutions of social work intervention in relation to problems contracted for between client and social worker.[15]

It was apparent from the beginning that no significant changes in practice were possible without the commitment of the professional staff. The early applied studies demonstrated that changes occurred because the staff worked with the researchers from the time the first question about practice was raised to the point when they examined the findings and recommendations together.

In initiating its first step toward professional accountability, the Department of Social Work Services had to consider its own design in relation to the medical institution's goals and objectives. The Department had gained the right to set its goals and guidelines for services (by and with its professional staff). It did so with the master's degree in social work as the governing professional direction. While the Department held to its identified goals, its professional staff members had not been educated either to the professional tenet of "social contract" or of accountability; as students training for a profession, they had been taught ideas of social policy in egalitarian terms but not standards of professional practice. As Fizdale noted, their socialization was job-oriented and not professionally determined.[16] Clark suggested that achieving professionalism was more an "article of faith" than of education for quality practice through theory-based learning.[17] Both administrative and staff attitudes and behaviors had to change in order to encompass professional accountability for practice, to develop professional maturity.

The development of departmental purpose and objectives was initially set in a statement of philosophy, translated into operational and functional dimensions. That beginning forced an early look at the practice and the changes needed. An essential first step in the examination demanded a staff development program which would better prepare the staff for its self-identified status: the achievement of self-direction. The self-directing worker, it has been stated, functions with a conscious sense of and commitment to accountability to the client system (patient and family), to the Department and the medical institution, to the reimbursing and regulatory bodies, and to the profession itself.[18] This commitment requires a continuous re-examination of all aspects of his or her practice in the social health setting, with concurrent self-expectation for continuous learning. Enhancement of practice is considered essential to the consumer's interest. Staff and administration together had recognized that successful learning was neither lodged in nor limited to one-to-one —or even group—supervision. All agreed that professional continuing education should be an open, mutual learning and teaching experience deriving from all resources within the institution, including staff colleagues, and that the social worker must actively seek out opportunities for his/her own education.

In addition to establishing attitudinal criteria, it is essential to determine performance criteria and standards. Department's and staff's responsibilities in the assessment had to be determined and the content and the methods for achievement provided. At Mount Sinai, the professional staff and its leadership now deal with all aspects of quality and quantity assurance. Each of these developments meant moving from personalized, subjective determinations to attempts at objective analyses. As well as seeking objective measures of practice evaluation, there was concern for consumer responsiveness and provider satisfaction to services delivered as further means of judging the outcome of practice. The assumption was that satisfaction was a factor in outcome and that attitudes, motivation, and satisfaction are closely related to each other.

This book concerns the major issues in professional accountability for social work in a hospital setting. Its contributors have drawn on their experience to examine these issues in concept and in a practicum "how-to."

In setting the direction for this study, the editor attempted to assess the current climate and the historical developments regarding professional responsibilities, accountability for quality of care, and efficiency in delivering services. She posits that the federal legislation and regulations imposed on medical care settings catapulted the providers, including social workers, into evaluation of their services and identifies the process for social work to meet the mandate.

Paneth and Lipsky develop social work's place in utilization review, assuming a key role for it. The underlying assumption for social work services in the social health care setting is predicated on the social-psychological-environmental dislocations resulting from illness or disability requiring hospitalization, and the special needs of patients and families to cope with these stresses as critical outgrowth of or contributions to physical stresses. The authors support the validity of social work involvement in utilization review since its beginning at the hospital, claiming for social work the responsibility for sound discharge planning and a concern for effective utilization of beds, i.e., validated hospitalization. With promulgation of the recent federal regulations, P.L. 92–603, social work moved quickly to develop its own system of early case-finding based on high social risk. The early Berkman and Rehr study had demonstrated "late" entry into social work services based on the referral system.[19] Early case-finding meant that social work could offer assistance with all or any of the problems encountered as a result of being hospitalized. By entering situations early, social work could treat hospitalization as the transitional phase it is and begin to call on patients and families for the resources and strengths that they will require to support their post-hospital needs. Throughout, Paneth and Lipsky emphasize the meaning and understanding of social-emotional factors of the ill in relation to others, especially doctors and nurses who deal with each hospitalized day of the patient. The collaborative process is the sine qua non for achieving both comprehensive and quality care. Paneth and Lipsky translate the demands of the new regulations into new organizational arrangements, which also affect the social work system. Social workers must learn to work with others, to deal with internal and external system and bureaucratic requirements, to find their positions in the system at key times and places, so that the individual patient-family situation becomes optimized and comprehensive.

Rosenberg and Rehr offer a background in statistical maintenance, in quantitative assurance and analysis, and in the structural needs to secure these. They describe differential approaches to quantity factors, interpreting the significance in structural accountability. The authors state their preference for a uniform statistical maintenance system, with institutional specificity yet capable of covering a region of health delivery systems. They describe the Mount Sinai social work services data system and consider what it can offer in terms of analysis of patient and provider profiles in the delivery system. A sound data base, with retrieval means to cull relevant information, affords all of staff, the administration of the Department and of the Hospital, the responses to all questions on "who," "what," and "by whom given," so that the interpretations lead the staff to judge changes for the improvement of services.

Alma Young's work with chart notations, the backbone of all reviewing systems, moves from the early case discussion methods for exchange of information and planning (common to psychiatric and medical rounds) through the rationale for annotating the medical record. Because the medical record is the daily repository for meaningful information, the medium of exchange among the key actors in the patient care system, and the historical legal documentation of a significant episode in the patient's life, Young validates social work entries to the chart. Social work has a contribution relevant to the daily care of the patient, bringing an understanding of his social-environmental lifestyle and his patterns of behavior to diagnostic formulation as well as to treatment direction. The exchange among treating agents changes perceptions and relevancies of the care, and unquestionably affects planning for post-hospital care. Modern

social health services with multi-professional and interdisciplinary requirements make the chronological written statement
the tool of exchange.

Young asserts that the quality of chart entries is predicated
on the growing security of the social worker as a professional. The
enhancement of quality is revealed in sharpened assessment and
treatment skills, heightened utilization of interdisciplinary exchange, and enhancement of the social worker's collaborative
expertise. Each new health care professional must undergo this
process and the sound entries that are its results. Experience and
continuing education advance the social worker's ability to communicate in clear, concise chart entries, to demonstrate the ability to meet the mandate to document services, and to do so in a
professional manner. Most workers find the structural demand
for chart entry a way of refining their assessments. Young describes the development of a medical chart notation system for
social work entries, a major first step in professional accountability for social work in health care. The entries serve the many
purposes cited, but in addition they are the major component in
peer review for assessment of practice: chart notations are assumed to indicate the quality of practice delivered.

Development of a peer review system is described by Chernesky and Young. The assumptions governing the practice of the
professional staff are promulgated by that staff; they are: that
good social work intervention is substantially different from bad;
that a chart notation can be an indicator of quality of practice;
that social workers can assess the quality of colleagues' work; and
that professional review, when utilized with professionals, can
contribute to improved clinical services.

The peer review system demonstrated again that structure
was needed in order to implement a review system. The staff
had to revise existing means and to develop new tools in order
to monitor quality of care. The earlier work on the development of chart notations served in good stead, both as the model
for working on the problems and in providing one of the assessment tools. A group process, however, must take place before
professionals willingly assume responsibility for review of peers.
Chernesky and Young show that the staff can introduce factual
and evaluative methods and utilize them in the review of others, that professionals can review the work of professionals. The

reviewers must be of a professional caliber respected by peers: insightful, critical yet objective, clear and fair, acknowledging the good as well as the bad. A good review system permits a peer "comment." Quality comments serve as a continuing educational prod for the recipient. An overall quality rating is a simplified summary, familiar from our past school experiences. However, use of a rating system requires retraining of staff, since social work's traditional evaluation system is descriptive. Joining rating with comments appears to be a helpful approach, and the overall rating system serves the Department in its overview of practice.

Chernesky and Young tell us that a peer review system has, as its first benefit, early and acknowledged improvement of the reviewers' own practice and chart notations. They ask if rotation of staff to assigned reviewing responsibilities should be considered, but the need for continuous training of reviewers limits the recommendation for rapid turnover. As the data become clear and more feedback to individual practitioners occurs, the staff's needs to improve clinical and collaborative skills become apparent. Information is examined by the Department in its nameless totality, and practice and structural changes are raised by staff review of the whole. As the system advanced, the staff's concern with assumed structural impediments to practice changed to mention of their own continuing educational needs.

This peer review system has not achieved anonymous review, but it did demonstrate in time that "knowing the worker" did not affect the chart assessment. The most important asset of the peer review system is its feedback loop, which identifies present and potential problem areas and the expectation of dealing with them. This is done for the individual practitioner; the system lends itself to overall review, or to audit of given topics or areas of practice. As developed and modified by the Mount Sinai social workers, however, the peer review system is extremely expensive; it takes considerable time from the reviewers and makes heavy administrative demands. All agree that efficiencies and other approaches to peer review must be sought, while all participants praise what it has achieved in professionalism.

Rehr and Berkman develop a rationale for their approach to an audit of social work interventions in a health care setting. The source of the data is the social worker's perception of "contract" with client and outcome, stated on a prescribed questionnaire placed in the medical chart, in conjunction with a statistical maintenance reporting system. They state that, to engage in an audit, certain constants are essential: a valid and reliable data collection system, a means of retrieving what is needed, and established norms, criteria, and standards against which to assess practice. A systematic approach to input is required; the system designed at Mount Sinai calls for the use of the Berkman-Rehr social problem classification system. This chapter draws on the key findings of the first Social Health Care Evaluation (social work audit) done at Mount Sinai, to establish a methodology for internal audit. The authors describe the use of the problem-contract approach, worker judgment on outcome, and client follow-up on the worker's perception. They comment on the high correlation of agreement between clients and social workers on the problems dealt with and their outcomes, and they demonstrate that the social problem approach is a device which can readily be incorporated into the medical record of each patient who has received social work services. The social problem classification for health settings has been validated, and is an inexpensive means of annotating judgments at a point in time. The audit has probable interdisciplinary application. The authors believe, although it still remains to be tested, that the social work audit can be undertaken by non-social work medical record staff, as has been done for Medical Care Evaluations (MCE); professional interpretation would need to be applied to the findings. Given the training of staff in uniform approach to completion of schedules, the social work audit has cross-institutional application, and a regional review could deal with a range of delivery questions. In the experience at Mount Sinai, the audit as devised does not gather the same information as the peer review system, which lends itself readily to both process and outcome assessment. The audit deals with outcome in relation to "contracted" social problems and can draw on structural and statistical factors as well. Statistical determinants could, however, be built into peer review. At this time, both approaches to professional review are being developed so as to improve the staff's professional accountability measures.

Rosenberg develops the components and the different stages required by different manpower in preparing for professional accountability. He initially correlates professionalism and the self-directed worker. He brings together peer review and self-direction, assuming that the development of opportunities for independence, for decision making, and for assessment of practice by the professional and his peers will lead to self-governed professional accountability. Rosenberg holds that the agencies and schools must offer opportunities in a range of continuing education programs to keep professionals relevant and current, meeting expectations. He describes a continuing education program which has grown out of the Department's changing philosophy and programs, evolving as it emerged side-by-side with chart notation, peer review, and audit developments. He notes how staff examines the practice dynamics they identify and then translates them into teaching-learning objectives. It is openly acknowledged that a faculty must be developed, concurrently, at least, as learner-teachers, committed to the objective of self-directedness—a major shift from traditional supervision. The new faculty goes through the same continuing educational opportunities, assuming practice responsibilities, developing their own expertise, their own clinical self-regulation, and teaching skills for practitioners who are now "on their own."

Content needs for further learning are revealed through peer review and audits, having been assessed by reviewers, and then incorporated into a feedback to staff. In this way continuing education becomes an ongoing process based on professional review measures. Rosenberg concludes by recommending that evaluation strategies are needed to test the staff's learning achievements and satisfaction.

The participants in the "adventure" are convinced that it is easier for the young, ready to enter practice, to assume professional responsibility in the terms outlined, than it has been for those who have had a traditional history of professional working style. We believe then that all the components in the Mount Sinai system must be opened to social work students so that they can be exposed to the same professional accountability demands as the staff. Caroff and Wilson delineate the students' exposure to a joint academic and field experience provided through the Hunter-Mount Sinai Social Work Consortium, in which students experience a wide range of service areas and types of situations in the different institutions of the Complex. The concept of preceptorship, involving a student with two or more preceptors, permits him or her to "see, hear, and feel" the practice of experienced social workers and to probe for the professional rationale in each case. In exposure to all aspects of the health care system, the climate for self-directedness is created, with the expectation of professional accountability to the institution, the consumer, and the profession a learning objective. The structural arrangements, the preceptor system, and the educational coordinators encourage independent learning habits, questioning of observed acts, and identification of what students need to know and where to learn it. Learning objectives are openly shared. Assessment of field and academic content in the context of learning objectives led to inclusion of mini-courses in the field, with a didactic emphasis, related readings, and a "reality" assignment. The "mini" serves to test content and responsiveness to such key areas as collaboration, peer review, and audit. This material has been incorporated into the overall health care module at the Hunter College School of Social Work.

The "record" is given its due at last, demonstrating its practice meaning. Students are taught the institutional requirements for written statements within guidelines, passing over the process record. The "record" is taught with clarity of purpose, explicitness, evaluative goals and plans, collaborative effort, community resources, and outcome. Written "process" has been replaced by other teaching tools, e.g., audiovisual tapes and one-way screens. The record is taught for what it is—the patient's record, and its purposes, with social work's contribution to it. The guidelines are comparable to staff expectation. Students who come in their second year must still bridge the gap between process and purposive recording, but once this is accomplished they acknowledge a sense of "more self-direction and independence in their thinking about the needs of the client and their interventions in meeting these needs."

Statistical data and time in relation to work patterns are used dynamically to teach essential quantifying factors in the structure of services, their productivity, their cost, the reimbursement sources, and the regulatory mandates. Students learn to use such data to answer questions in relation to improving practice. At present all students in the Consortium are involved in a pilot study, utilizing the Berkman-Rehr Social Problem Classification system and outcomes to service, in order to provide a social work audit experience.

In addition the students are exposed to utilization review methods, such as high social risk screening where they are taught to identify patients "at risk," to initiate an encounter without a referral request, to develop an "agreement" for services, and to assess a service area for social work need. In all, collaborative relationships and assessment techniques are highlighted. These efforts link the students strongly with the health care system, not with the client system alone. The proximity to the medical school permits special conjoint teaching/learning experiences for students in social work and in medicine, exposing each to different disciplines dealing with the same client system.

An accountability system is professional only when professionals are involved in making it so. From the beginning the Department's staff was and remains involved in the commitment to quality assurance. In Chapter 10, social workers describe the meaning of professional accountability to them and its effect on their practice and their sense of professional self-directedness. Topper, Zofnass, Smith, and Parsons describe the staff's involvement in early case-finding, in contracting as a practice development, in outcome and audit, and in beginning with peer review. Their perceptions show that the assumption of professional accountability enhances professional acumen, skills, and practice, while it supports client-related values and ethics. They recommend program change and continuing education based on the results of peer review and audits.

In looking to the future, Rehr has high hopes for social work's assuming professional accountability for practice. She examines the Mount Sinai experience and its broader implications for the field of social work in health care. Mount Sinai staff and administration have demonstrated that they can undertake an "adventure" resulting in professional and program gains, that "good" care can be delivered, and that it is recognizably different from "bad." However, she does not underplay the problems that professionals continue to face in their search for quality assurance.

Rehr evaluates the experience for social work directors attempting to find a rightful place in institutional programs, and to enhance social work's programs in health settings. In addition, she sees that the self-directed worker using quality assurance measures is the primary participant in reordering of direct services that are more meaningful to clients, and improve the worker's skills in delivering care.

Rehr predicts changes in the future of health care services and their meaning for social work, urging the field to examine current experiences and interpret the findings for tomorrow's practice, citing documented social work service, information systems, auditing, and peer review as quality assurance tools to improve professional practice. She also prepares social workers to include the consumer in the assessment process and the profession's requirements to achieve a knowledgeable, good interaction between consumer and provider.

Finally, Rehr advocates regionalization of social work services, as a more effective way of planning and programming for given populations. Within a regional program, however, she allows for the uniqueness and the autonomy of each institution and department. She urges all of us—professionals, associations, schools, departments of social work—to take part and contribute to the quality assurance adventure.

References

1. National Association of Social Workers, *Guidelines for Assessment,* Washington, D.C., Preface.

2. Morton L. Arkava and E. Clifford Brennan, "Quality Control in Social Work Education," in *Competency Based Evaluation for Social Work,* edited by M.L. Arkava and E.C. Brennan, New York, Council on Social Work Education, 1976, p. 8.

3. Frank W. Clark, "Characteristics of the Competency-Based Curriculum," in *Competency Based Evaluation for Social Work,* edited by Arkava and Brennan, p. 28.

4. NASW, *op. cit.,* p. 2.

5. *Ibid.,* p. 5.

6. Harold Lewis, "Standards in Social Work: Implications for Practice and Education," Unpublished paper, 1974, mimeographed, pp. 18–19.

7. Eveline M. Burns, "Rethinking Accountability: External and Internal Pressures," Keynote address, Alumni Annual Conference, Columbia University School of Social Work, October 29, 1977.

8. Helen Rehr, "Professional Standard Review and Utilization Review: The Challenge to Social Work," Presented at Conference on Social Work and PSRO-

UR, Society for Hospital Social Work Directors, Ft. Worth, Texas, January 18, 1976.

9. E.M. Burns, *op. cit.*

10. Ruth Fizdale, *Social Agency Structure and Accountability,* Fairlawn, N.J., R.E. Burdick, Inc., 1974, p. 162.

11. *Ibid.,* p. 162.

12. *Ibid.,*

13. Helen Rehr and B.G. Berkman, "Social Service Casefinding in the Hospital —Its Influence on the Utilization of Social Services," *American Journal of Public Health,* Vol. 63, No. 10, October 1973, pp. 857–862.

14. Barbara Berkman and Helen Rehr, "Social Needs of the Hospitalized Elderly: A Classification," *Social Work,* Vol. 17, No. 4, July 1972, pp. 80–88.

15. Barbara Berkman and Helen Rehr, "Social Work Undertakes Its Own Audit," *Social Work in Health Care,* Vol. 3, No. 3, Spring 1978, pp. 273–286.

16. Fizdale, *op. cit.,* pp. 162–163.

17. F.W. Clark, *op. cit.,* p. 28.

18. Helen Rehr, "Accountability: For What? To Whom?" presented at the Ninth Annual Meeting, Society for Hospital Social Work Directors, American Hospital Association, Atlanta, Georgia, 1974.

19. Barbara Berkman and Helen Rehr, "Unanticipated Consequences of the Casefinding System in Hospital Social Services," *Social Work,* Vol. 15, No. 2, April 1970, pp. 63–78.

2

The Climate is Set for Quality Assurance: Implications for Social Work

HELEN REHR

Review of delivery of care is not new to medicine or to nursing. Flexner's report on medical education in 1910 was essentially a review of contemporary medical care. Long before that, Florence Nightingale had done an assessment of nursing care given war casualties during the American Civil War. Both studies led to changes. As early as 1912, E.A. Codman systematically reviewed hospital services, devising the term "end result" of care delivered for assessment.[1] Since Flexner and since the development of professional nursing, there has been a commitment to patient care assessment in medical institutions. Evaluations have been by means such as mortality review, tissue or pathology review, and surgical review committees. These reviews were initiated to uncover questionable situations, occurring as a result of an individual practitioner's rendering of care. They were, essentially, performed as peer reviews, although they were internal reviews and handled within self-determined institutional guidelines. The professionals and the institutions together protected themselves from outside pressures.

In 1957, the Joint Commission on Accreditation of Hospitals (JCAH) was created, with the responsibility for reviewing hospitals in the United States. It was formed by the four major professional organizations: the American Medical Association (AMA), the American Hospital Association (AHA), the American College of Physicians (ACP), and the American College of Surgeons (ACS), to create an independent structure which would establish an accreditation program to review hospital facilities.[2] The initiative was directed at the assumption that structural standards, governing manpower and their qualifications, facilities and physical environment, service provisions, and internal reviewing mechanisms afforded the means and the opportunity for quality care delivery.

But quality assurance review shifted from a voluntary to a required activity with the enactment of the 1965 amendments to the Social Security Act. There had been an earlier attempt in the fifties to review medical care when the federal government supported a community-based medical review program, Experimental Medical Care Review Organization (EMCRO), in its attempts to define standards for delivery.

Provisions of Medicare, Medicaid, and special Children and Maternal Health Services legislation required that facilities which were to be reimbursed for care to the beneficiaries of these programs must be subject to review. The review was to be undertaken by an agency acting for the federal government; the responsibility could be assumed by the JCAH or by a state-based agency. In any event, a Utilization Review Commission was also required to review regularly the "necessity" and "quality" of services. The federal government's growing financial investment as a provider of services through its own systems—veterans' programs, military and public health services, and as third-party payer for services to the poor, the elderly, the special-disease afflicted, and special children and maternal needs—caused it to couple the concern for quality with that of cost containment.

The mandate for peer review and audits occurred because of the failure of the professions and the institutions to monitor their own actions or to implement their findings. Most quality controls have been forced on the medical care establishment in response to abuse, misuse, or waste, or in questionable expectations concerning reimbursement, particularly from Medicaid and Medicare.[3]

A rash of laws and regulations followed when the cost of programs under Titles 18, 19, and 5, and of health care systems in general, expanded beyond all predictions. In 1972 P.L. 92–603 established Professional Standards Review Organizations (PSROs) and End Stage Renal Disease (ESRD) with the means to review the appropriateness and the quality of services. The PSRO provision was developed "to promote effective and economical delivery of health services of proper quality for which payment may be made under the Act."[4] Inherent therein was the assurance of "proper utilization of care and services—the maintenance of skills and the need for the physician to have up-to-date knowledge."[5] While this reference is specific to physicians, it is also applicable to non-physician practitioners.[6]

The emphasis moved in 1974 to utilization review as the primary mechanism, compatible with the PSRO provision, representing the "in-hospital" function review. The aim was to establish norms, standards, and criteria in relation to admission and length of stay in hospitals, as well as concurrent review methods and the development of a Uniform Hospital Discharge Data System (UHDDS) for Medicare, Medicaid, Title 5, and ESRD patients. Then followed P.L. 93-641, the National Health Planning and Resources Development Act (NHPD) which created the Health Systems Agency (HSA) structure. Consumers and providers are expected to assume local health planning responsibilities. Inherent is the expectation that either HSAs or state health planning agencies are required to have a sound data base in order to meet their planning needs. The data is expected to be available from the providers themselves. Then came P.L. 93-353, the Health Services Research, Health Statistics and Medical Libraries Act of 1974, in the hope of creating a Cooperative Health Statistics System (CHSS) with a coordinated data mechanism. The intent was to link all the health regulations in a single system with the flexibility to answer national and specific regional needs, while it captured data called for under UR, PSRO, NHPD, and others, within some structure provided via the National Center for Health Statistics under which the CHSS law was launched. All agencies are being asked to cooperate with each other.

The current demand for information and data reflect how little is known about the nature of health services and to whom they are provided. If individual institutions or systems are aware, the knowledge is usually self-contained, in their own sets of definitions and data gathered. There is little cross-institutional evaluation nor is anything available that could be collected for regional health services planning. Health information systems have not kept up with changes, nor are they prepared to deal with demands to be made on them. There is no routine or uniformly collected data; there are no uniform definitions or labeling for items. At the very least, comparable, uniform data are needed, covering: (1) demographic information; (2) admission and discharge dates, diagnoses; (3) facilities, services, and manpower utilized; (4) utilization data such as length of stay, visits, diagnoses, occupancy-service ratios; (5) costs, charges, budgets; (6) reimbursement patterns by all parties. Developing a uniform data bank with access to readily retrieved information is no simple undertaking. The most cherished concept is that data are one's own private preserve. The threat to "autonomy"[7] is proclaimed, suggesting a fundamental incompatibility between quality and cost containment expectations. There is the belief that government review or expectation through peer review is an abrogation of professional responsibility, that enforced monitoring may cause physicians to "lose professional accountability to public accountability."[8] Information governing clients or patients to be used for assessment at the individual level is regarded as a break in confidentiality. "The conflict is between the right of the government and the public to information and the right of the individual to privacy."[9] These concerns are real enough. However, information is already available and documented on all citizens for many things. The true issue is data utilization under sound structural arrangements. While the potential for abuse does exist, the nature of monitoring in the public interest is at stake. The problems of implementing any system, national and regional, are substantial, including political difficulties. The questions of "who" should operate data banks, "how much data are enough," "how and where should they be stored," "who has access to them" and "control of them" confront the designers, as well as questions of confidentiality and privacy.

The expectation in most professional reviews, when they are not explicit for planning, is to assure that health care (physician and non-physician, whether acute hospital care or long-term care) is necessary and consistent with professionally recognized standards, as well as with the medical needs of the patient. That care is expected to be of quality, and cost-contained. Whether through PSRO, state-based agencies, ESRD reviewing bodies, or other designated regulatory groups, it is expected that the services delivered will be reviewed. The review is to cover the institution, the physician and non-physician providers, and patient profiles, to evaluate the quality of care rendered by the individual practitioner and the quality of care provided by the

medical institution. These demands on providers have required
the establishment of reviewing mechanisms to cover:

— Professionally developed and recognized norms, criteria, and standards
— A data retrieval system to generate profiles on patients,
practitioners, and the institution
— A utilization review system covering admission, continued stay criteria, and medical care evaluation (MCE)
studies at regular periods
— A peer review system, ongoing and systematic, by which
professionals actively engage in appraisals of the practice of peers, in accordance with stipulated criteria
— Mechanisms to correct identified deficiencies related to
an individual practitioner's performance and to organizational factors
— Continuing education of professional providers to improve services, based on the findings
— Uniform information and data systems to provide regional and cross-institutional assessments[10]

Such a quality assurance program is a system for continuous
self-examination by an institution and by those professionals who
directly provide the care (physician and non-physician providers). All efforts at monitoring quality require the strong support
of the professionals and of the consumers, who receive the services purchased through third-party agents. Quality assurance
addresses professionally determined standards of care, and includes ongoing systems of monitoring, evaluation, and corrective
action. Efforts to assess quality service fall within the broad area
of evaluation: where and at what to look, how and what to measure, with still undefined standards and times for measurement.
Further possible and probable interrelationships are accessibility
and availability, continuity, comprehensiveness, manpower, organization of services, patient attitudes, provider attitudes, compliance and education, consumer satisfaction, commitment, and
continuing education.

The problems in evaluating health and hospital care are
multiple. Social work, along with all other health care professions
in medical institutions, faces critical and unresolved issues in

quality control. Donabedian suggests the range of factors that may affect these issues:

a. How does one define health? Would it be in physical, physiological, psychological, or social functioning terms or in some combination?

b. How does one define the instrumentalities to health? Would it be in the models of practice as in individual practitioners, groups of providers, or in a system of providers?

c. How does one define the client system? Would it be the patient served, his family, a caseload, or a target population?[11]

The issues call for different questions, techniques, and approaches for review, and for development of relevant standards and criteria.

While the literature reveals that much is known about quantity measurement, even in limited and fragmented form, the real difficulty is measurement of quality assurance. Judgment of the practitioner in his direct service to his patients is usually viewed along three dimensions: structure, process, and outcome. If it is assumed that structural standards affect outcome of practice, then judgments must be made about the quality of the facilities, equipment, staffing, qualifications and experience of personnel, organizational arrangements, information system, and financing which are available to support the service delivery. Of late, a number of these variables have been reviewed to determine if a relationship exists between structural standards and quality of care. "It was believed that a good structure would inevitably lead to a good process and hence, good outcome."[12] However, studies have not always confirmed a linear relationship between the two. There is some correlation between good processes and good facilities, but structure standards alone are not sufficient as an assessment of quality. Structural assessment, however, possesses the advantages of highlighting internal organizational arrangements and the organizational, administrative, and manpower arrangements which affect delivery. It is not uncommon to find organizational impediments to care when medical care evaluations (MCE) are performed.

Process standards viewed in relation to outcome examine the "services, activities or events that occur relative to patient care."[13] The purpose of process assessment is to determine how appropriate, how valid, how skillful were the judgments made by the practitioners. What is done to and for the patient and the basis for these acts is the subject of process evaluation. There are limitations in this method when it is introduced without relation to other means of measurement.[14] The resources available to the practitioner in order to deliver care and the total complexity of that unknown—the patient-recipient—constitute the full process.[15] In addition, most health care is multi-professional or multidimensional, making its tracking difficult. Process assessment has the advantage that procedures, modalities, interventions on behalf of patients can be described or defined—very frequently, counted and aggregated. One way of regarding the process performance, including time and number factors, is that it may be assumed to be related to skill and experience.

The third factor, outcome, is considered the ultimate validator of quality of care. Outcome describes the results of the care provided based on an evaluation of the given status or selected aspects.[16] Outcome, the sine qua non of indicators, is the most difficult to measure. By *what, when,* in *what terms, by what definitions, how,* and *by whom* is it to be judged? Should it be looked at in physical, mental, behavioral, or economic terms? Outcome, it is generally agreed, is a complex and expensive route to determine quality of care. Intervening variables are many, and there is always the problem of whether the outcome was actually due to the factor claiming it: controlled studies with good research techniques permitting matched samples and randomization of treatment inputs are extremely difficult to apply in clinical situations. Assessment, as currently promulgated, cannot yet analyze the clinical judgment drawn upon by the individual practitioner, yet this is a key factor in the quality of process and outcome. Evaluation can deal with provider satisfaction and with the practitioner's response to his own performance; however, subjectivity is inherent in this type of analysis. Nevertheless, provider judgments have been used in viewing outcomes and reflect some validity in assessment and in peer review.[17] In spite of the limitations in securing outcome measures, considerable work is under way in this area now, and "what happened" is being addressed in specific terms. Consumer satisfaction with services received is one possible route. The difficulty in this type of assessment is to secure uniformity in response, to get the same reference points for all who are interviewed. Furthermore, it is necessary to cope with subjectivity in individuals' judgments. Nevertheless, utilizing the consumer's response to the care he has received together with the provider's judgment of what he gave can provide some correlations relevant to the delivery of care.

The mandate for quality assurance measurements has major implications for social work. Quality assurance demands come at a time when the profession is greatly concerned with the services it provides. As has occurred in all the helping professions, the question of the effectiveness of social work has been raised. Critics abound while others quietly proceed with serious and constructive efforts to respond to accountability. Evidence of the profession's interest in greater self-regulation may be found in the way it has embraced the PSRO mandate in the health care field. Social workers, as one group of non-physician health care practitioners, are expected to be involved in peer review, and in audits of the medical institutions in which they practice. They have also been included in the local, state, and national levels of PSRO, and other reviewing bodies. The National Association of Social Workers and the Society for Hospital Social Work Directors (SHSWD) of the AHA have lent their leadership at national and regional levels by developing and projecting structural standards, reviewing methods, and designing continuing studies to assess the quality of care that social workers deliver.[18]

The NASW, through its Committee on Health Quality Standards, recently completed its study of social work quality assurance programs already existing in the health care field. Coulton's analysis of those programs reinforces the basic requirements and the general trend toward promoting social work's professional accountability in health settings.[19] The Council on Social Work Education is also seeking standards for competency-based education, as evidenced by its publication of the University of Montana's study in this area.[20]

The implications are far-reaching and call for substantial reorganization in professional and administrative relationships, in new roles for social workers, in utilization review demands, in case-finding, in new skills and interventions, in new programs, in enhanced collaboration, in commitment to continuity of care, and, finally, in developing professional evaluative and accountability measures. A new professional social worker, committed to and socialized into the profession, assuming full responsibility and accountability for performance and for outcome of his services to the people he aids, stands just ahead.

The complexity of the problems remains. Are social workers to stand still or to continue the search? All approaches to date are better than none at all. Waiting for the perfect model means none now. The route is one of trial and error, which means controversy and difference but also new knowledge. Though the very existence of pluralistic models of care—the American antimonolithic style—complicates the reviewing techniques, no one has suggested that we give them up, only that we improve them. It is clear that reviews cannot cover everything—all tasks, all judgments, all personae in any situation or under any circumstances. They can, however, examine identified problems, specific to professional knowledge and skills, problems which are amenable to some currently available intervention, to assist the individual, and then the aggregate of individuals.

Quality assurance is here to stay, whatever its auspices. While many problems remain, the effect of reimbursement has made in-hospital quality assurance a required activity, covering structure, process, and outcome, eventually to encompass all social health care, and assigned to a system with the responsibility for quality control. Voluntary methods such as JCAH, specialty boards and professional associations, grand rounds, clinical conferences, internal review committees may—and should—continue but in the final analysis, quality assurance is a necessity. Just preparing for the numbers is staggering: "30 million hospital episodes, almost a million nursing home admissions, and up to a billion outpatient transactions per year."[21] The prospect demands at least common and uniform data banks, federal funding assistance, a strategy for demonstration, research, training, and evaluation. The complexities of translating the needs to local levels are yet unknown, but cooperation, linkages, and political support must be sought. A major undertaking is already under way.

References

1. End Stage Renal Disease Program Guidelines, Health Standards and Quality Bureau (HSQB), Department of Health, Education, and Welfare, 1977, p. 1.

2. *Ibid.,* p. 2.

3. Lowell E. Bellin, "Supervision of Health-Care Watchmen—By Whom?" in *The Professional Responsibility for the Quality of Health Care,* 1975 Annual Health Conference, Bulletin of the New York Academy of Medicine, Vol. 52, No. 1, January 1976, pp. 16–21.

4. PSRO Program Manual, U.S. Department of Health, Education, and Welfare, Office of Professional Standards Review, Washington, D.C., U.S. Government Printing Office, March 15, 1974, p. 1.

5. "Medical Education in the United States," Department of Medical Education, AMA, *Journal of American Medical Association,* Vol. 226, 1973, p. 896.

6. PSRO Program Manual, *op. cit.,* p. 12.

7. Margaret A. Wayne, "PSRO: Issues in Health Care Policy" *Health and Social Work,* Vol. 2, No. 4, Nov. 1977, p. 38.

8. *Ibid.,* p. 39.

9. *Ibid.,* p. 42.

10. PSRO Program Manual, *op. cit.,* Section 703.

11. Avedis Donabedian, *Aspects of Medical Care Administration,* Cambridge, Harvard University Press, 1973, pp. 58–207.

12. Richard Greene, *Assuring Quality in Medical Care,* Cambridge, Ballinger Publishing Co., 1976, p. 24.

13. End Stage Renal Disease Program Guidelines, Chapters 301, 302, 303, Health Standards and Quality Bureau (HSQB), Department of Health, Education, and Welfare, 1977, p. 5.

14. B. Starfield, "Health Services Research: A Working Model," *New England Journal of Medicine,* Vol. 289, No. 3, 1973, pp. 132–136.

15. J.S. Gonnella, and C. Zelenik, "Factors Involved in Comprehensive Patient Care Evaluation," *Medical Care,* Vol. 12, No. 11, 1974, pp. 928–934.

16. End Stage Renal Disease Program Guidelines, *op. cit.,* p. 5.

17. R.H. Brook, and F.A. Appel, "Quality of Care Assessment: Choosing a Method for Peer Review," *New England Journal of Medicine,* Vol. 288, No. 25, 1973, pp. 1323–1329.

18. See *Development of Professional Standards Review for Hospital Social Work,* Chicago, Ill., American Hospital Association, 1977, and *Standards for Hospital Social Services,* NASW Policy Statement 6, 1976, Washington, D.C., National Association of Social Workers, Inc.

19. Claudia J. Coulton, "Social Work Quality Assurance Programs: A Comparative Analysis," prepared for Committee on Health Quality Standards, Washington, D.C., National Association of Social Workers, 1978.

20. M.L. Arkava, and E.C. Brennan, *Competency Based Evaluation for Social Work,* New York, Council on Social Work Education, 1976.

21. Michael J. Goran, "The Future of Quality Assurance," *Bulletin of the New York Academy of Medicine,* Vol. 52, No. 1, January 1976, p. 180.

3

"Utilization Review" and
Social Work's Role

JANICE PANETH
AND HANNAH LIPSKY

Utilization review has been undertaken with increasing momentum since the enactment of Titles 18 and 19 of the Social Security Act, which became effective in July 1966.[1] Prior to that time, utilization committees had been developed in about 20 percent of United States hospitals. These committees, in the main, were instituted in response to the requests of insurance companies for some control over the use of hospital beds and hence their expenditures. However, there was also concurrent concern for such review with regard to quality of care.

Title 18, the Medicare amendment, was specific in mandating utilization review as a requirement for a hospital's participation in the program.[2] The standards required that the hospital have in effect a plan for utilization review which applied at least to the services furnished inpatients entitled to benefits under the law. An acceptable utilization plan provided for:

1. Review on a sample or other basis of admissions, duration of stays, and professional services furnished
    and
2. Review of each case of continuous extended duration

The standards were also specific in regard to the organization of utilization review committees' methods of functioning, records, and so on. It is significant that this milestone legislation, involving government participation in obtaining hospital care for people 65 and over, included requirements to influence the delivery of those services.[3]

At The Mount Sinai Hospital, the Medical Board's Utilization Committee originally defined extended stays as those of 30 days or more. Over time, until July 1975, when new federal requirements became effective, the review period changed, and physicians were requested to recertify their patients every 14 days. In addition, spurred by the high occupancy rate and the demands for beds, the Committee undertook to review "emergency admissions" (patients whose life-or-death situation required immediate admission), and "relatively urgent admissions" (patients whose situations required admission within ten days) to determine whether the patients admitted under these classifications met the specifications. Moreover, the Committee early extended its purview to review the stays of all patients at the Hospital regardless of funding source.

The Department of Social Work Services has held membership in the Utilization Committee since 1966. In addition to regular review with the Committee of the status of extended-stay patients, the Department's functions have included:

1. Participating in interpretation of changes in the legislation as these may affect patient care
2. Providing the Committee with information regarding the availability of community resources
3. Contributing to the development of the Committee's policies and procedures
4. Meeting with representatives of external reviewing organizations

The Utilization Review Committee quite naturally expected the Department of Social Work Services to effect discharge plans for extended-stay patients; the Department's dilemma concerned its simultaneous responsibility to patient and family to work out discharge plans as effectively as possible. It was clear that the Department could not undertake the role of "enforcer" of length-of-stay expectations, yet the Department shared the concern for effective use of hospital beds, recognizing that prolonged hospitalization was not in the patient's interests, and keenly aware of its shared responsibility for the expenditure of public funds.[4]

In time it became possible to achieve a balance among these concerns. The Department established a prompt and regular reporting system on all inquiries from the Committee. The Committee responded to the need for early referral of social work services, by acting as a forum for such discussions and by communicating with colleagues; the regular inquiries to physicians as to the reasons for further stay included provision for referral to social service.

The social work service staff, after initial uncertainty, recognized that their prompt responses to the Committee's referrals and requests for information were a keystone in establishing an effective working relationship. In turn, the Committee was responsive in accepting the judgments of the social work service staff with regard to the need for continued stays in individual situations.

A major area of the Department's function developed simultaneously with the initial 1966 participation in the Utilization Review Committee. The Board of Trustees officially recognized the need to extend social work services to private patients and approved additional staff positions for this purpose. It had been expected that it would be necessary to undertake a campaign of interpretation to the attending staff in order to effect referrals. However, experience proved this step unnecessary; attending physicians rapidly became a growing referral source, and the case load became quite full and changed rapidly.

During this period the Department also reviewed the use of master's level professional staff, and developed a social work assistant program, at the bachelor's degree level, to implement many of the specific tasks involved in discharge planning and in obtaining the necessary entitlements and resources from a network of governmental and community resources in a variety of locales. A subsequent development was the Social Work Discharge Office, first called the Transfer Service, designed to provide a more effective and efficient means of channeling information and resource availability to the Department's staff and to provide current information and documentation of the Department's inter-institutional referrals, delays in transfers, reasons for such delays, and the like. The Office serves as an ongoing device to measure, in part, availability of resources, and effectiveness of the systems internally and externally.

Amendments to Regulation V of the
Social Security Act

The current phase of the Department's participation in utilization review was prompted by the amendments to the Social

Security Act passed by Congress on November 25, 1974, affecting the use of acute hospitals and nursing homes. In New York State, compliance was expected as of July 1, 1975. The regulations stipulated:

1. The validity of every admission to the hospital must be certified by the designee of the UR Committee within 24 hours of admission, or in pre-admission. This means that every admission is reviewed in accordance with explicit criteria for every diagnosis regarding indications for admission.

2. At the time the admission is validated, the predicted length of stay is assigned, based on data for the average length of stay for particular diagnoses. These data have been gathered by the American Hospital Association (the PAS System), the New York State Hospital Utilization Review (NYSHUR), and Blue Cross.

3. A discharge plan must be projected within the first seven days of hospitalization and the chart annotated accordingly.

4. The original predicted length of stay must be validated within 24 to 48 hours of its expiration. Extensions of the original length-of-stay prediction must again be validated by explicit criteria and endorsed by the UR Committee. When a stay is not extended, the patient, the physician, the hospital, and the funding agency must be notified. Stays beyond the validated period will not be paid for by the funding source, and the regulations provide that the hospitals cannot bill the patient.

5. The development of at least one medical care study, as a retrospective review of care given in the institution, must be in progress at all times, and one study must be completed each year.

The new regulations and those that followed vested the government with powers of enforcing cost containment and of monitoring criteria for admission, transfer, and discharge, and also included specific qualitative criteria for continuous and regular self-auditing of professional care. The regulations called for testing of professional values and standards pertaining to patient care as a hospital moved to compliance.[5]

Hospital Preparation

New York State granted the hospitals six months to prepare a plan of compliance with the new regulations. The Mount Sinai Hospital took the following steps:

a. The Utilization and Review Committee of the Medical Board created a task force to design systematic methods.
b. The task force redesigned the pre-admission and admission sheet. This had to be approved by the Medical Board.
c. A utilization and review plan for the Hospital was created.
d. The task force undertook orientation and education of the interdisciplinary staff.
e. URMA (Utilization Review and Medical Audit) Notes were published to inform the collaborative staff of changes and progress.

The task force consisted of one representative from administration, medicine, admission office, utilization and review nurse, home care, and social work services, all of whom were staff directly involved in the process. Their first effort was to design (1) a pre-admission and (2) admission sheet which would provide diagnoses and indications for admission from which the utilization review nurses could project lengths of stay. The Hospital has utilized the length-of-stay norms of the New York State Department of Health Utilization and Review (NYSHUR).

Since the new regulations required that discharge planning begin prior to the seventh day, social work needed to select much earlier than formerly those cases for which service might be needed to effect discharge within a specified time. It was suggested that discharge be recognized as an interprofessional function. The concept of triage for discharge was transferred to similar collaboration at admission. Early intervention was viewed as vital for high quality discharge planning. Identification of the socially vulnerable early in their hospitalization implied change in social work practice. Therefore, the Department urged that the Hospital include on its pre-admission sheet social data which could be used for developing social work's high social risk determinations. We asked the physicians who requested admission for their patients to respond to the following questions:

1. Does the patient live alone? With spouse? With spouse and young children?
2. Does the patient live in a hotel? Rooming house?
3. Will patient be able to resume usual functioning on discharge?
4. Will patient require assistance at time of discharge? At home? Elsewhere?

Such information, together with the diagnosis(es), the age of the patient, and the projected length of stay would indicate the need for immediate screening.[6]

The utilization and review plan which was published and sent to the Medical Board, to chiefs of services, and to all attending physicians included such items as by whose authority the plan was determined, the organization of the Committee, and the Committee's functions. It is a dynamic plan which not only calls for a review and an analysis of the NYSHUR data but for continuing changes based on the continued stay review; the plan has proved flexible enough so that the new legislation which followed could be absorbed and implemented.[7]

Once these pre-admission and admission sheets had been designed, the entire medical staff, and the physicians' secretaries as well, had to be acquainted with the implications and the use of these forms in admitting patients. It should be repeated here that there are three types of admissions to this 1,200-bed hospital: (1) emergencies, that require admission within 24 hours, (2) relatively urgent situations, that can wait up to ten days, and (3) elective admissions, patients whose admission can be planned (usually surgical). Sixty percent of Mount Sinai's admissions are elective. Doctors present the information to the Admission Office, and the patient is given a date for admission.

The request for information as to whether patients lived alone met with some resistance from doctors and doctors' secretaries. More than 100 of the latter had come to discuss the information now required when they called in to the Admission

Office. Initially, they thought social information not pertinent, and several stated that the physician did not know the patients' living arrangements. They left with the understanding that the patient's discharge to his home is frequently dependent on the social supports available.

These orientation sessions occurred at various levels—in staff meetings and in administrative conferences. The speakers were representatives of administration, utilization and review nurses, social work, and home care. In addition, Mount Sinai began to publish Utilization and Review and Medical Audit Committee Notes (URMA notes), which orient all staff to the new regulations and continue to provide feedback and information on the progress being made in implementation of the program.

Design and implementation of the program were performed on a collaborative basis, and this ongoing planning process has contributed largely to the program's success.

Discharge Planning

Where regulations required the naming of a specific discharge coordinator, it was a natural development at The Mount Sinai Hospital for this designation to be made within the Department of Social Work Services.[8] For many years this Department has functioned with the philosophy that quality discharge planning is an important aspect of social work function, that such planning requires the collaboration of the health care team, and that social work is uniquely able to enlist the patient/family in determining the individual plan. It is the Department's conviction that the scope of social work can provide a sense of continuity and comprehensiveness from pre-admission functioning, through hospitalization, to after-care readjustment with a major commitment to the individual patient and family lifestyle.

At the same time, Department members have been aware that this point of view has not been universally shared within the profession. Often it is viewed as an obligatory task, beset with regulations, procedures, and forms—a requirement which must be met, to enable social workers to practice other, more valued functions. The authors call attention to this bias, convinced of the ever-increasing importance of social work's contribution in this area. Work and skill are required to provide effective service to a variety of patients, with a multiplicity of social problems, who are experiencing crisis. Discharge can be viewed narrowly or broadly. In the broader view, the role of discharge planner will be fought for by the social work profession and acknowledged by others when there is recognition of the role that social factors play in maximizing health, in responding to and in maintaining the benefits of treatment.[9]

For most patients, hospitalization is a short-term crisis, an interference, and a temporary assault which may have either no effects or far-reaching effects on social functioning or social roles. Discharge planning includes:

1. Identifying high psycho-social risk patients in order to initiate beginning assessment
2. Contracting with patient/family and helping them to become participant members of the health care team
3. Collaborating with other professions in care of the patient, learning from them the nature of the illness and its prognostic implications, and keeping them informed of the social work assessment of the patient and patient/family struggles with the information they are receiving, and patterns of coping
4. Ongoing work with the patient and family as they cope with the illness
5. Reassessing the patient's and family's adaptation to new realities of social and physical functioning, either temporary or permanent, with the implications of role change at home and at work
6. Providing viable choices in the coping process, mobilizing resources and connecting with outside systems to mesh with patient's/family's/doctor's plan of care
7. Testing the validity of the plan and determining new needs in after care

To work successfully at these tasks within a specified time limit, the social worker needs skill in individual and family treatment and skill in working with the collaborative network. Several modalities of treatment can be used. Ability in assessment and treatment of trauma and loss are required in order to translate these toward achievement of integration and readjustment within a short period of time.

Practice Implications
for Social Work

The need to comply with the new regulations became an opportunity to examine social work practice within the Hospital in a critically constructive way and to effect important changes. Earlier studies of such practice had shown the Department's dependence on other personnel to identify those patients/families requiring social services and social work's entry into situations late in the patient's hospitalization.[10] The nature of planning at this time required social workers to become responsible for identifying their own case load. A series of strategies made possible intervention with patients in the early days of their hospitalization and now, also, dealing with the impact of illness and of hospitalization on patient/family, as well as early planning for post-hospital care.

In order to effect these changes, the following steps were taken, not necessarily in the order cited. Some were done seriatum; some, simultaneously:

1. Identification of high social risk criteria pre-admission
2. Identification of high social risk criteria at admission
3. Early intervention by social work in high social risk identification cases (within 48 hours after admission)
4. Establishment of a policy of assigned intake
5. Staff development and practice change as a result of the above
6. Participation in social work audit in relation to social problem classification
7. Periodic refinement of high social risk criteria and appropriate deployment of staff
8. Identification of long-term stay review and discharge planning criteria
9. Implementation of validation study of high social risk

Pre-Admission Assignment

It was possible to review the pre-admission sheets and offer service, prior to admission, to those patients selected as having a high degree of social risk. These were identified as patients coming into the Hospital for a type of surgery which might impinge on their social functioning upon returning home, those who lived alone, or those who had small children for whom planning would be helpful. While patients in the lower socioeconomic level were regarded as having possible vulnerability, high social risk was not limited to that group.

The program began in July 1975, manned by a professional social worker, who called the patient within the ten days prior to admission, suggesting knowledge of the fact of the admission —not the illness—and exploring with the patient the need for social work services either in relation to anxiety about the illness, or for concrete services to help the patient plan his admission to the Hospital. Examples of assistance offered ranged from: a visit to the Hospital for a young person, entering for surgery, who had never been in a hospital before and was extremely frightened at the prospect; homemaking services to hospitalized mothers of young children; assurance of help to elderly people living alone that they would be helped to return home with some assistance if necessary; specific suggestions to out-of-state families for housing, for transportation to and from airports, for linkages back to their own homes; meeting individual needs of handicapped patients entering the Hospital; and enabling patients to raise additional questions with their own doctors.

The telephone as a medium of exchange prior to admission was not always successful; not as many patients as anticipated could be reached. Therefore this part of the program was dropped after one and a half years, because of Department financial problems and staff deployment needs. There was almost 100 percent acceptance and appreciation for the call; even when a patient did not see the need for social work service he felt the Hospital's concern for him as an individual. Pre-admission information was placed on the medical chart, and the interview served as a bridge for beginning intervention by the social worker assigned to the service.

Identification of High Social Risk
Leading to Assigned Intake
at Admission

In order to initiate practice change with staff who had become accustomed to obtaining referrals from the collaborative staff, in

December 1975, a policy of assigned intake was set up, using high social risk criteria and recommending to staff that it pick up these cases within 48 hours after admission.[11] The policy of pre-admission screening for elective cases was accompanied by criteria for admission screening for cases coming in as emergencies or as relatively urgent. Clusters of illness which have to do with social risk were delineated:

1. Illnesses which are life-threatening; these include second- and third-stage cancers, and other illnesses such as meningitis
2. Illnesses which presume change in physical functioning, e.g., gastric surgery which may result in colostomies, fracture of limbs, stroke, severe heart problems, brain tumors, laryngectomies, vascular problems, and gangrene leading to amputation; illnesses which may presume temporary or permanent loss of sight, hearing, or speech
3. Illnesses having to do with change in body image, e.g., head and neck surgery
4. Chronic illnesses, such as asthma, lupus, arthritis, myasthenia, leukemia, multiple sclerosis, cerebral palsy, Hodgkins, ileitis, colitis; patients who have had multiple admissions

To these criteria were added out-of-state patients, particularly those coming from a considerable distance.

A non-professional staff member was assigned and trained to identify the illnesses categorized by the above concepts and to mark staff admission sheets accordingly, noting the need for priority pickup. Staff was asked to screen these cases within 48 hours after admission, or as early in the hospitalization as possible. A small percentage of the patients on the service entered the social work system later on: patients who came in with a minor diagnosis and became at risk, or patients whose behavior or social problems during hospitalization could not be identified on any admission sheet.

Concurrent with the above, a staff training program of 4 one and one-half hour meetings was begun. The first session dealt with the overall regulation, its implications for social work, and social work's ongoing involvement in the quality assurance pro-

gram. Two sessions included presentations of case material highlighting the shift in practice when a social worker is involved
early in the admission of a patient. These shifts in practice had
to do with the style of entry when a social worker is involved with
a non-referred patient and must explore the need for ongoing
social service using professional knowledge of the social determinants in the patient's illness; a shift in the collaborative role, in
which the social worker entered the case long before the doctor's
perception of social need. Although staff now had criteria by
which to enter a case in order to assess the need for ongoing
service and/or discharge planning, it was understood that it
would immediately share this assessment with the patient's doctor to obtain from him the implications of the patient's illness,
and to keep him informed of the reasons for social work entry.
This initially affected some of the medical staff and will be discussed later.

The fourth session had to do with ongoing audit of outcome
and an assessment of ongoing staff development needs in relation
to the shift in practice.

Part of staff development had to do with discussion of the
philosophic and economic base on which these regulations were
projected. Other regulations, from city and state, resulting from
and correlating with the federal regulations, were beginning to
affect staff as well. The audit, discussed in a later chapter, was
helpful to staff in concretely demonstrating the services they
offer and clarifying the perception of their professional role by
the consumer of their services.

Impact on Staff and on Practice

The development of high social risk factors as applied to social
work assessment and treatment bore heavily on staff both quantitatively and qualitatively. What evolved quantitatively was the
need for refinement of high social risk factors, using social workers' professional knowledge of specific illnesses and social and
emotional problems. In addition, workers were encouraged to
use various practice methods such as chart review and consultation with nurses on social supports in order to determine priorities for in-person interviews. It became clear that the criteria of

high social risk required refinement. Administratively, it was possible to identify those areas in the Hospital which uniformly had the greater number of high risk patients and to plan redeployment of staff in densely high risk services such as neurology.

Qualitatively, there was a shift in the time factor when cases were picked up. Two-thirds of the situations identified as high social risk were picked up in the first week of hospital stay which made a very different demand qualitatively on the social work services offered. Social workers had to look at the many stress points that accompany illness and affect both patients and families; separation from home, impact of hospitalization, the procedures leading to diagnosis, impact of fluctuations of the illness, role change from person to patient, and from patient to person again with the return to the community, the crisis of impaired personal functioning on the patient's family, discharge and aftercare to enhance social functioning within the family, coping with exacerbation in chronic illness.

With the movement of the social worker into the patient's room within 48 hours after admission, non-referred, uncertain of the patient's need for services, the social worker found it awkward and frequently distressing to get started. Heretofore, there had been the referrer's request. The new training focused on patient/family's functioning prior to hospitalization and how hospitalization and the current series of crises were affecting the ways in which patients and their families were coping.

Staff development of an intensive nature was needed, both one-to-one and in seminars, to teach how to enter with the knowledge of the patient's diagnosis, his age, his living alone, or the presumption of disability, and how to begin relating to a patient who is feeling ill, undiagnosed, uncertain of the meaning of the many tests, and unaware, sometimes, of the implications of his hospitalization. The timing of intervention shifted, but the overall purpose—a clear understanding of a patient/family and how the illness was perceived and coped with—remained the focus. Early intervention and the ongoing relationship offered would lead, it was believed, to facilitating individual patient/family discharge planning. Various methods of approaches were tested: listening to tapes, attending seminars, role playing, and feedback to the staff in how it was contributing to the health team's knowledge to enhance patient/family care.

The workers recognized that this led to a deepening of their practice and a greater appreciation of their collaborative contributions. Nevertheless, they expressed constant irritation with the assigned intake policy since they felt it restricted their autonomy. They argued that doctors' diagnoses on the admission sheets differed, to some extent, from their experience of what was happening to the patient, and that teaching the collaborative staff, particularly nursing, the concept of whom to refer to social work services was one of the positive roles that they established in determining the needs of patients. The problem of autonomy is under discussion and the staff is now working with a combination of methods, including assigned intake, to select those patients requiring service.

One of the positives in the approach was a change in the collaborative relationships with doctors. Although a few doctors objected to social workers entering a situation without their prior approval, there was recognition by most that such early intervention resulted in prompt and more effective discharge planning and that increased participation helped them with their patients and families to maximize the benefits of medical care.

After a year or more of determining its own case load in partnership with the doctors, using criteria of social risk factors on admission, staff has already gone a long way, although with some degree of awkwardness, in its change of practice. High social risk determinants have been further refined, and established with the staff on the basis of its experience with the initial stages, fully considering their own patterns of collaboration. Staff has developed the following conceptual framework for identifying high social risk: A study was conducted in April 1978 to determine whether these criteria are valid. Based on the findings, the criteria are now being revised.[12]

Manpower Deployment

Over the years, a rule of thumb for the deployment of social workers has been the ratio of social workers to the number of beds. Over the years, too, the experience of the profession has been that there is little reliability in this ratio as an indicator of need for social work intervention. Effective staff deployment requires additional information, such as: Who in a sociodemographic sense are the patients who occupy those beds? How long do they stay? What are their medical and social diagnoses and treatment plans? What are their physical and social limitations? What are their post-hospital needs? What resources are available to them? All of these social concerns affect the Department's philosophy and program of services available.

The use of various data-gathering devices provides the Department with some guidelines for deployment. The high social risk screening instrument (Exhibit 1) identifies those Hospital service areas which are apt to have a larger number of such admissions, and hence require staff equipped for early assessment. The use of length-of-stay prognostication is also a guide for staffing, since experience and study to date show extended stays as a clear indicator for intervention.

Another indicator for staff assignment is obtained from those services whose patients are more apt to require post-hospital concrete services—either help in the home or in an inter-institutional transfer. These data provide the base not only for the numerical assignment of staff, but also for the levels of staff to be utilized. While quality discharge planning is the province of skilled social work, it is evident that a number of tasks required to effect the plan can be specifically identified. Once identified, these tasks can be variously assigned to social work assistant or clerical personnel, thus extending collaboration within the Department. This method also furthers the administrative obligation to achieve currency with legislative and regulatory requirements and to develop Departmental practice and procedures accordingly, and assists the dissemination of resource information and experience.

The data bases used for these methods of staff deployment are evolving. They do not relieve staff of pressure, but they do provide a means of equalizing that pressure. They do not identify all patients, but they provide a rational base from which the profession can proceed to develop its knowledge of areas of need and to act and plan accordingly. They also provide the Department with information required to deploy its staff so that it can meet its responsibilities to the institution in effective regulatory compliance.

Continued Stay Review

Although the social worker identifies high psycho-social risk in order to enter early in the patient's hospitalization and attompt to discharge within a designated length of stay for the diagnosis, this arrangement does not cover every patient within an acute hospital. It does not include those patients whose admission is due to a series of symptoms requiring exploratory diagnostic procedures which subsequently uncover a high social risk diagnosis, nor does it include the patient who comes in with a simple diagnosis, a short length of stay, and is later discovered to have a more serious underlying illness for which treatment must begin and a new length of stay determined. The arrangement cannot include an individual patient's reaction to treatment and medication which at times makes recovery within a designated time limit impossible. For these reasons, it is necessary to find strategies of collaboration with the utilization and review nurses, strategies shaped by historical relationships and the nature of the interface with utilization review.

Ideally, collaboration begins on the service level. At Mount Sinai, as at many institutions, social workers are expected to initiate and develop collaborative rounds with nurses and residents on a weekly basis. These rounds may occur as walking rounds, as review of cardex, may concentrate on new patients, "difficult" patients, and patients whose discharge appears imminent. The rounds serve as an outlet for each professional to discuss the patient/family current status within the expertise of his knowledge. The discussion may include difficult behaviors, the patient/family social situation, the impact of illness, and impediments to discharge; it is a holistic approach to an understanding of the medical, functional, and social status of patient/family and enables the group to plan accordingly. The utilization review nurse and the home care nurse are also members of this team. The latter uses discussions to identify potential need for home health services; the utilization review nurse reads the chart notes by physician, social worker, and nurse, correlates this information with insurance coverage for either patient or Hospital in compliance with state and federal regulations, and raises questions about current status and future planning.

In addition, the utilization and review nurse identifies the over-40-day patient and provides a list of these to the discharge coordinator. (In Mount Sinai, that individual is in social service.) This list is furnished monthly on a report form designed by the discharge coordinator. Each social worker is then requested to provide information as to the patient's admission date, date opened in social work, date (if known) when the patient will be ready for discharge, and social work assessment and plan. The report, a collaborative effort by utilization and review and social work, provides an administrative accountability measure to determine: (1) whether the long-term stay patient has been picked up by social work and how soon after admission; if not picked up, the reason; (2) whether the patient is remaining for medical reasons, and (3) if the patient is remaining for social reasons, for what reason. The staff understands that, under the federal regulations, if a Medicare patient remains because of the need for a skilled nursing facility placement, Medicare will continue to pay. If the Medicare patient remains in the Hospital for other than SNF placement, New York State Medicaid has stipulated that it will pick up coverage when application has been made to at least five institutions or when the delay in discharge is due to the inability of the Medicaid system to process the applications for post-hospital Medicaid eligibility. The report therefore alerts the staff to compliance with these regulations. The long-term stay review alerts the social worker, the preceptor, and the discharge coordinator to situations where especially careful chart documentation is required so that the Hospital may be fully reimbursed.

On another level, collaboration continues between the discharge coordinator and the utilization review nurse. They submit a monthly report to the Utilization Review Committee of the Medical Board which provides the number and the status of the long-term-stay review cases. At the monthly meeting the Committee uses the opportunity to question the reasons for the delay. The discharge coordinator identifies to the other professionals the "hard to place patients" for medical and social reasons (e.g., the coma and/or the alcoholic patients). This report serves to underline the current inability of the state and city to act efficiently in determining eligibility for Medicaid. These are factors of which the physicians on the Utilization and Review Committee may not be aware, and the information can help to mobilize their efforts for change.

The Department has an additional tracking system relation to placement of patients in another institution for any level of care. Through a centralized procedure, one social work assistant transmits all the required forms to the designated facilities and/or funding agency, and continues by tracking receipt of the forms at various institutions, following up by means of regular telephone contacts, and keeping the appropriate social workers informed of bed availability, reasons for delay in placement, and so on. This social work assistant provides a monthly report to the Department which gives information on the number of patients placed, the medical department where they received their hospital care, the length of time required to effect placement, the names and types of other facilities used. Recently, the Department has begun compiling similar information on home health services.

In reviewing reports on long-term-stay cases for the year and in correlating timing of the social worker's entry into the case, social work staff clearly has a beginning expertise in detecting the patient socially at risk. Conversely, in a number of instances a social worker has clearly decided that intervention is not required. This growing data base for an efficacious patient identification system, plus the regularity of information interchange in both short- and long-term review, mean that collaboration with the utilization review staff is firmly rooted and available as an instrument in program development.

The factor of cost containment is of course the basis for much of the utilization review legislation, and the authors share the general worry and concern regarding rising costs and effective use of resources, and believe that the measures described contribute to cost containment. Manpower assignment based on areas of need and skill level required is one positive contribution. Another is social work's assistance in the reduction of unnecessary hospital stays—in its financial aspect only, apart from the obvious benefits to patient/families. It is difficult to attribute reduction in length of stay to any one factor, but reviews of patients' charts by funding agencies have indicated the successful effects of the Department's early intervention, since there has been little if any questioning of continued length of stay for social reasons.

Accomplishments and Implications
for Social Work

In considering Mount Sinai's utilization review program, the following steps have been accomplished:

— The use of a high social risk screening mechanism enables social work to identify its own case load.

— Early identification in turn makes it possible to work with the impact of separation and hospitalization and to effect quality discharge planning.

— Social work is an effective participant in the Hospital's planning to meet new legislative requirements and regulations.

— Social work makes an important contribution to cost containment, by validated lengths of stay, early planning for post-hospital needs, and data-based deployment of its own manpower.

The authors believe that utilization and review carries these additional implications for future planning:

— The emphasis on shortened stays, which will continue and increase in numbers, places a strain on social work ethics and values in the effort to comply. Social work must be a vigilant advocate of patient choice in discharge planning, and in assuring patient/family participation and informed consent.

— Current regulatory requirements and computerized procedures are making ever-increasing inroads on confidentiality, which necessitate constant monitoring.

— The profession requires continued education in the political process in order to strengthen its efforts with a variety of governmental officials to humanize policy and procedures and to develop careful methods of documenting and collecting information regarding gaps in community services for continued efforts to bring about government programs to meet identified needs.

— It is necessary to refine the high social risk at-admission criteria and develop the identification of high social risk ambulatory patients for the purposes of health education and maintenance.

— Continuing education concentration must be extended to the post-hospitalization period and the re-stabilization of the patient within the community. Also, although the Department's experiences with chart notations are detailed in another chapter, it is important to develop the ability to write notations which contribute to collaboration and comply with regulations and funding requirements.

The authors seek to balance what has been accomplished by what needs to be done. Nonetheless, important steps have been taken, using the regulations as a springboard to enhance professional practice and hence the contribution to good health care.

References

1. John Rumsey, "Utilization Review Committees: Statement of the Problem," *JAMA*, Vol. 196, June 13, 1966, p. 994.

2. Standards of Conditions of Participation, published in the *AMA News*, January 31, 1966.

3. Barbara Berkman, "Utilization Review—A Synthesis of Current Medical Thinking," Unpublished paper, July 1, 1967.

4. "A Guide to Social Work Participation in Utilization Review Process in Hospitals." Monograph of the United Hospital Fund of New York, August 1966.

5. "Discharge Planning for Hospitals," publication of the American Hospital Association, 1974.

6. Barbara Berkman and Helen Rehr, "The Search for Early Indicators of Social Service Need among Elderly Hospital Patients," *Journal of the American Geriatrics Society*, Vol. XXII, No. 9, 1974.

7. "Utilization Review and Medical Audit in the Health Care Institution," statement of the American Hospital Association, 1975.

8. Discharge Planning Guidelines—Interim. New York State Department of Health Division of Health Facilities Standards, July 1976.

9. Kathy C. Forrest, Position Paper on Hospital Discharge Planning, American Hospital Association Society for Hospital Social Work Directors, May 1977.

10. Helen Rehr, "Quality Assurance: Issues for Social Services in Health," in *Proceedings: Quality Assurance in Social Services in Health Programs for Mothers and Children*, edited by William T. Hall and Gerald St. Denis, Pittsburgh, Pennsylvania, April 1975, pp. 35–53. The Institute was planned and implemented by the Joint Public Health-Social Work Training Project MCH #114 and with financial support from the Bureau of Community Health Services, HEW Contract # HSA-105-74-83.

11. Forrest, *op. cit.*

12. Helen Rehr, Barbara Berkman, and Gary Rosenberg, "High Social Risk Screening—A Validation Study," paper presented at the 106 annual meeting of the American Public Health Association, Los Angeles, California, October 16–19, 1978.

4

Quantity Assurance and Structural Standards

GARY ROSENBERG AND HELEN REHR

Many professionals think the collection and utilization of data are a threat to the creativity of their practice. Many administrators of social work services in health care or other settings lack experience in securing data and may be intimidated by information if it arrives without interpretation of findings and recommendations. These same administrators and practitioners have depended on research consultants to interpret the agency's work and the staff's practice. Frequently practitioners have protested against the interpretation of study findings by those not actually involved in the practice. A basic deficit has existed in the orientation and training of many service professionals—not social workers alone—in the awareness and utilization of information and data to enhance practice and the administration of a program.

Even if information and data are limited to the individual practice, they are essential to each practitioner, to review what has been done in one case or a number of situations over time. Questions must be asked regarding the client(s), the agency's goals and structure, the resources available, and the individual practitioner. An administrator interested in the agency's or department's program over a period of time, must know who was served, in what way, by whom, how, when, and where, and, if possible, the outcome. Both practitioner and administrator seek reliable information and data to make judgments, decisions, and determinations about different developments which may be essential to enhance practice or program.

The information essential in dealing with direct services on behalf of clients includes a number of factors common to one case or to a number of cases in one worker's case load, or in the department's total direct service work load. Some of the questions likely to be asked are:

— Who was served in sociodemographic terms, and, as important, who was turned away?
— How did the patient/client get into the social service system of care?
— At what location (from within or without) was the patient/client at time of entry?
— What was asked for?
— How was the patient/client perceived?
— What service(s) was given? To whom? By whom? Over what period of time? How frequently?

The questions can become more complicated, particularly when the questioner asks "what happened" and who or what was responsible for the outcome; the answers to more complex questions call for definitions and measurements still unresolved: where to look, at what to look, how, when, and what to measure. These latter issues are factors in quality assurance.

Much is known about quantitative assessment, despite its limitations, the lack of uniform collection methods, and the lack of clarity in definitions. Data collection systems have been described both as accountability tools and as management information systems to help with management decision making. Too frequently the systems are regarded as the means by which staff's productivity and performance alone are being measured and therefore are suspect to the practitioner. The authors believe that data and information systems form the bases from which to secure a wide range of answers to practice and program questions. By utilizing quantitative data appropriately, criteria for practice can be translated into standards. In end-stage renal disease review programs, for example, the criteria for a psychosocial assessment of patient/families who are being considered for a renal transplant are translated into an acceptable standard in the 90 to 100 percent bracket for all situations.[1]

Even though no uniform systems yet exist to collect national or regional data in the health care field, many purposes and benefits may be realized by maintaining reliable information and data collection systems within the single institution and social work department. Some of these purposes are:

1. To determine the need for and contributions of social work services

2. To study the kinds of patient [and family] services that are needed
3. To assess staffing needs of the social work department
4. To provide a measure of accountability to the hospital administration, the clients, the social work profession, the third-party payer, and the government
5. To aid in budgeting and cost accounting
6. To serve as an administrative tool.[2]

Furthermore, such information can serve professional standards review—including utilization review—and permit program assessment. Frequently overlooked is the fact that the components to items 1. and 2. can offer practice enhancement answers to the practitioner; what is learned can serve:

7. As a basis for continuing education of staff, and for determining changes in the program to permit improved services.

These two last objectives constitute fulfillment of regulations mandated under new federal law.

Numerous systems exist for detailing quantitative accountability. The major differences among them are whether these systems count units of time or direct services to patients and families, including supportive services, collaborative contacts, and telephone interviews.

Vanderwall suggests that the accountability of social work must address itself to five levels: (1) the source of its financial support; (2) the agency which determines the allocation of resources; (3) the profession and its standards; (4) the particular program's goals and objectives; and (5) the consumers of the services.[3]

Bard has designed a quantitative system similar to that of Vanderwall, including opening data and weekly sheets, and collection of data on services given as compared to goals set for the month.[4]

Rehr articulates the position for a uniform data base for a region:

— Common denominators are then available; while standardization can be achieved, flexibility in the use of different programs and practices is possible

— Systematic shared study methods become more readily possible for:
  a. determination of social needs of patient populations
  b. determination of the services needed to meet these needs
  c. assessment of the services rendered
  d. the determination of sound program priorities in service

— Working in groups, on both administrative and on worker levels, when not limited to one setting, could be strengthened and would allow for comprehensive interpretations of data to hospital administrators, boards, consumer groups, third-party payers, the profession

— A uniform system should be helpful in determining from where demand is coming at given points in time, and thus be helpful with aspects of staff assignment, program planning

— Cost assessments could be jointly determined, differences would be understood and program could be interpreted as a regional approach to the delivery of services[5]

A regionalized approach to assessment of delineated services makes a uniform statistical system with uniform collecting methods paramount for quantity assurance.[6] The common denominators in any of these uniform data-based systems consist of an opening, transfer/closing, and daily data-gathering forms. Daily input safeguards the currency and accuracy of the information. The automated system gathers data on direct, supportive, and telephone contacts, and a measure of client satisfaction can also be presented. Rehr also demonstrates how applied studies, including outcome, are generated by these data.[7]

Vielhaber and Irvin describe a semi-automated data-gathering system. They state these advantages over the traditional manual system:

1. It conserves professional time; individual social workers are not required to complete case activity reports manually.

2. Information is available in a central file shortly after a case is opened and no clerical processing (such as typing) is required. The worker also retains access to the information while serving the patient and/or family.

3. Data elements may be modified easily by simply changing the items on a four-part form and printing a revised version. Since library computer programs are being used, no additional specific programming is required in order to account for changes in format. We expect to modify our version periodically in order to meet changing data needs.

4. This system is inexpensive, relatively simple to use, and may be easily modified to meet the needs of different hospitals. The essential elements that are required are forms, preparation, support and access to a computer

facility with library programs. Lengthy training in the use of the system is not required; staff members need only to be instructed in a few rules for using the four-part form.

5. Timely statistical data of a wide variety are available for purposes of program management, planning, evaluative research, and in estimating allocation of professional time.[8]

They stress the quantitative data as providing the base for process and outcome studies.

Spano has developed a quantitative system, linked to a management-by-objectives framework. Included in his system are a problem classification system,[9] and a goal attainment scaling as an outcome measure. Spano and his colleagues have influenced the field to examine the results of direct services qualitatively.

Volland at Johns Hopkins has developed a system which identifies cost centers and gaps in services.[10]

Birdwhistell has also developed a computerized data collection system, which offers information by patient location as well as extensive patient sociodemographic data.[11] The advantage of Birdwhistell's work is that it identifies manpower needs by uncovering the volume demands in specific hospital locations.

Chernesky and Lurie have described data-gathering instruments which measure time inputs by allowing the system to translate direct and supportive services into time units.[12] The advantage of this approach is that it permits costing out the defined service while securing quantitative measurements of services provided.

Another data-gathering program for effective management has been designed by Elpers and Chapman in their information system for mental health services. Additional principles of data collection are suggested by these authors:

1. Data should be collected and processed for an explicit purpose; data should be collected to provide a basis for management decisions.

2. Although designed for managerial purposes, it should be meaningful to the entire professional staff. Management's commitment implies an acceptance of accountability for meaningful planning, and a desire to communicate with community and funding sources. It forces a concern for program effectiveness and for the best utilization of resources.

3. The management information system cannot be an isolated activity, but must be integral to the planning, monitoring, and program innovation processes.

4. For data collection to be adequate, summary reports must be fed back to the organization in a form that is clearly useful and timely.

5. In order to minimize the burden of data collection, various requirements for clinical, administrative, legal, financial, and other information should be combined as much as possible so that one form can serve multiple purposes.

6. The design of a management information system requires a combination of talents—clinical, research, management, accounting, clerical, form design, and data processing, to mention a few. Design must proceed on a number of fronts simultaneously: definition of variables coding, clerical feasibility studies, data processing requirements, report content, and the like.

7. Personnel at all levels should participate in the design process. Not only is this essential for the system to be acceptable to the people that must work with it, but personnel at all levels have useful contributions to make. While there are some general principles that must be observed in designing any such system, a management information system must be customized to the particular setting.

8. Establishing a management information system is not an overnight process.[13]

Rosenberg has contributed to information system design by offering a computerized data collection system linked to the problem-oriented record and goal attainment scaling, i.e., quantitative information linked to process and outcome studies.[14] Rosenberg's work has particular value for social work in the mental health field as well as in other health care programs: it carries interpretations across professional lines by using language common to all the behavioral fields and professions.

On October 26, 1977, "HR-3," the Medicare, Medicaid Anti-Fraud and Abuse Amendments, were passed by the Congress. This group of amendments changed the regulations regarding uniform accounting systems. "For the purpose of reporting the cost of service provided by, of planning, and of measuring and comparing the efficiency and effective use of service in hospitals the Secretary of Health, Education and Welfare shall establish by regulation a uniform system of reporting of . . . the cost and volume of services for various functional accounts and sub-accounts."[15] It is expected that the regulations promulgated will include the social work services in health care. Whatever data collection system for social work interventions is finally chosen, it must be readily adaptable to all hospitals and their departments and should be cost-effective in so far as the cost of instituting the system should not be more than the potential saving. The system will be expected to measure some product or defined output; time, although obviously meaningful in determining costs, is not likely to be acceptable as an output measure. The data systems currently being sought by the DHEW regulators do not ask for quality judgments but for counts of quantity and production in relative value units. The system selected, however, should be capable of measuring costs in relation to volume. These new federal regulations underscore the need for a data collection system with uniform adaptability to social work services in health settings, an issue considered by the Committee on Administrative Practices of the Society for Hospital Social Work Directors, which has resulted in "A Reporting System."[16] This culls information common to all, yet allows individual departments to seek and secure information specific to their own needs.

An information system must have the potential to gather relevant data regarding:

1. Direct and supportive services to clients covering:
    a. patients who entered the system of care
    b. providers and the services rendered those patients
    c. problems dealt with and their outcomes

This information is required on a daily basis, translated to monthly statistics, then either to quarterly or semi-annual tallies and always to annual reports. It permits individual client profiles, individual worker service patterns, and tallies based on any clustering of services as well as for the overall department.

2. Intramural activities covering:
    participation in hospital committees dealing with program, policy, and planning functions
3. Community-oriented services covering:
    participation in any health-related programs and committees dealing with community organization, planning, and coordination
4. Educational activities
    a. social work staff-related
    b. continuing education (intra- or extra-mural)
    c. interprofessional
    d. social work student-related

     e. other health care professional and paraprofessional student-related

5. Evaluation program and applied research dealing with

     a. peer review   with their feedback loop to staff for program change and

     b. program audit   continuing education

     c. inter-professional or multidisciplinary audits

     d. special studies

Items 3, 4, and 5 may be collected as needed: monthly, quarterly, semi-annually, but not less than annually. The data collection system must be available to the worker for current input regardless of the information-gathering period. The data required can be scaled up or down depending upon the department's size and needs for reporting to others.

The Mount Sinai Hospital Social Work Data Collection System

The Department gathers its information by staff reporting of defined activities. The direct and supportive services offered to patients and their families are stored and reported through an automated data processing system. Activities dealing with intramural concerns, community outreach, education, and evaluation are recovered through periodic reporting on an "other activities" hand tally form. (See Exhibit 2.) Together, these offer the staff, the unit of operation, and the Department a substantial amount of descriptive information regarding the range of services and activities undertaken.

The automated data system operates on three forms completed by all practice staff who helped to create the system initially or are oriented to its use:

1. A "registration" form (Exhibit 3) which captures patient sociodemographic data, worker, and service information

2. A "daily transaction" form (Exhibit 4) for each staff member, which captures all social work, direct treatment, and supportive modalities for each client

3. A "change of status" form (Exhibit 5) which covers any change in the case such as transfer, closing, or new information regarding the client.

The information gathered daily is reported for each statistical month to each staff member and to an administrative unit; e.g., to pediatric for its use, to the Department as a whole for management purposes. The system offers a monthly listing of cases with activity patterns per case, per case load, giving location at opening; it includes services a worker performed for a colleague.

A ratio of direct-to-supportive services for the month and case movement in and out of the worker's load and the Department's can be reported. Workers receive a listing of active and inactive cases; length of inactivity of the latter are listed to spur closing of the group. A list of new cases opened, with specific sociodemographic information, along with the closed cases and their social service duration, is given each worker each month. A fifth report from the same input offers staff members the total case load list, with specific activity information for each client, and serves as a quick reference. These reports may offer means of developing comparability among workers and cases as well.

The worker, the unit administrator, and the administrative staff receive monthly statements of activity patterns. (See Exhibit 6.) This supplies information as to "what" was given and "by whom." All staff have been trained to provide the information and to read and interpret the data. The system also permits reporting of data for specified categories: e.g., the number of 65-year-olds and over receiving social work services and the medical services where they were found (this statistical report's purpose is to provide unit costs of services to the elderly). Since the system furnishes data covering those served, the service(s) received, and the providers of the service(s), the specialized information can be clustered as required.

To date the system captures information along defined lines of what was done but does not yet provide data regarding those who need the services but were not reached. The introduction of a case-finding instrument (Exhibit 7) uncovering patients with high social risk will permit the staff to understand the gaps in services delivered. Recently it has become possible to compare the Department's data with information retrieved for the ambulatory care patients as a whole; other such comparisons will be possible. This Department has developed a problem/outcome report (Exhibit 8) for each case on closing, which has been adapted for audit purposes. Social work audit has been conducted and reported to the Medical Center's Audit Committee.[17] The problem/outcome form will be incorporated into the system for all cases at closing. The Department has conducted a telephone follow-up of patient and family units served (Exhibit 9) in order to assess the client's response (satisfaction) to services received. Such an approach permits undertaking selective studies. (See Chapter 7, audit.)

Data collection is predicated on a set of common definitions for all input items, based on development by staff. Additional information can be added. The system does not capture "time" spent for each defined function; this Department prefers to utilize an occasional time study in order to secure that information rather than burdening the staff to "time in" each function. Periodic time studies permit "ballpark" cost allocation to the different services.

There are many ways to approach data collection. One alternate system of counting adds relative value units, on whose standards professionals have previously agreed, to the services or functions defined. Numbers for these units are assigned to social work activities based upon the relative amount of labor, supplies, and other factors (such as overhead, electricity, telephone, and the like) needed to perform the activity. The relative value of a service performed, it has been suggested, is determined by a weighted formula in terms of:

1. The technical or clinical expertise required for the service
2. The interactional involvement with the patient and others
3. Whether it is a direct or supportive service/communication.[18]

A data system is of paramount importance for accountability and quality assurance. Standardization within the profession can be achieved within and among hospitals only if data are comparable. The creative use of data systems can contribute significantly to studies on populations, as well as on individuals, to determination of goals for the Department in relation to patient population and to quantity and quality of services needed to plan and move

toward sound program priorities. Comparative data can assist
the comprehensive interpretations of hospital administrators,
boards, consumer groups, third-party payers, and professionals. A
data system, linking productivity, cost efficiency, effectiveness,
and outcome, is important to a social work program of any size.
The profession has recognized that departments of social work
services in health care settings can best serve this clientele under
the existence of minimal structural standards, which may well
affect the quality and the outcome of services to the department's and the institution's clientele. Although studies to date
have shown no correlation between structural standards and outcome, there is enough evidence in evaluations of programs to
identify the impediments to the delivery of services.

In May 1976 the New York City Task Force on Quality Assurance completed its review and the Metropolitan Chapter of
the NASW and SHSWD published jointly *Standards for Social
Work Programs in Short-Stay Hospitals.* There were twenty-two
standards promulgated which were modified and expanded by
the Conference on Social Work and PSRO-UR, in January 1976,
under the co-sponsorship of the Society for Hospital Social Work
Directors and the National Association of Social Workers, Inc.[19]
These twenty-five standards were finally reduced to eleven by a
working committee of the two organizations and published as a
statement of policy by the National Association of Social Workers.[20] (See Exhibit 10.) Recently the Joint Committee on Accreditation of Hospitals revised its standards governing social work
services in hospitals and has set minimal standards.[21]

While there are differences between the JCAH and the professional organizations' projections, there are also similarities. In
principle all agree that:

— Social work services shall be "readily" available to the
   patient, his family, or significant others
— By a qualified social worker with standards calling for:
   — a written plan for providing services, indicating the
      range and function and designed by a qualified so-
      cial worker
   — administrative accountability to the institution's
      chief officer
   — objective, scope, and organization of the program is

to be clearly delineated in writing and periodically reviewed, and must include a manual of policies and procedures, defining roles and responsibilities of the staff, and personnel practices

— adequate documentation of social work services provided in the patient's medical record

— adequate space, budget, and facilities to fulfill the professional and administrative aspects of the department

— quality control mechanisms permitting continuous review and evaluation of services provided to patients and reported *back* to the staff for implementing recommended changes

— continuing educational opportunities available to the staff based on evaluations of program and practice

Social work's critical responsibility in health care is to define the objectives and scope of the program in relation to the institution's objectives, in order to meet the essential social problems related to such care realistically in terms of the manpower currently and potentially available. No all-inclusive program is available without a full and qualified staff. Too often, social workers, concerned with the extent of social need among the ill, wish to offer more than resources permit. A realistic program, in writing, shared with the institution's administration and key medical and nursing staff, as well as with the social work staff, constitutes the criteria against which services and performance can be tested, and an information system linked to structural standards provides a major key to the assessment.

References

1. "Project to Develop Model Criteria and Standards for Care of End-Stage Renal Disease Patient," California Committee on Regional Medical Program, Inc., Box 6059, Oakland, California, July 1976, p. 50.

2. Society for Hospital Social Work Directors, "A Reporting System for Hospital Social Work," Chicago, Illinois, American Hospital Association, 1978, p. 1.

3. W.R. Vanderwall, "Accountability of Social Services in a Health Program —A Working Model," in *Accountability: A Critical Issue in Social Services,*

W.T. Hall, and G.C. St. Denis, Pittsburgh, Penn., Bureau of Community Health Services, HEW, 1972, pp. 46–60.

4. R. Bard, *Program and Staff Evaluation*, Washington, D.C. Education Training and Research Sciences Corp., 1971.

5. H. Rehr, "Models of Accountability," in *Proceedings: Quality Assurance in Social Services in Health Programs for Mothers and Children*, pp. 63–67.

6. H. Rehr, "Quality and Quantity Assurance: Issues for Social Services in Health," in *Proceedings: Quality Assurance in Social Services in Health Programs for Mothers and Children*, pp. 35–53.

7. B.G. Berkman, and H. Rehr, "The 'Sick-Role' Cycle and the Timing of Social Work Intervention," *Social Service Review*, Vol. 46, No. 4, 1972, pp. 567–580. B.G. Berkman, and H. Rehr, "Unanticipated Consequences of the Case Finding System in Hospital Social Service," *Social Work*, Vol. 15, No. 2, April 1970, pp. 63–70.

8. D.P. Vielhaber, and N.A. Irvin, "A Semi-Automated Case Reporting System for Hospital Social Work Departments," in *Proceedings: Quality Assurance in Social Services in Health Programs for Mothers and Children*, pp. 54–63.

9. R. Spano, T.J. Kiersuk, and S.H. Lund, "An Operational Model to Achieve Accountability for Social Work in Health Care," *Social Work in Health Care*, Vol. 3, No. 2, 1977, pp. 123–142.

10. P. Volland, "Social Work Information and Accountability Systems In A Hospital Setting," *Social Work in Health Care*, Vol. 1, No. 3, 1975, pp. 277–287.

11. M. Birdwhistell, "Reporting System," University of Virginia, unpublished, 1973.

12. R. Chernesky, and A. Lurie, "The Functional Analysis Study: A First Step in Quality Assurance," *Social Work in Health Care*, Vol. 1, No. 2, 1975–76, pp. 213–223.

13. J. Elpers, and R. Chapman, "Management Information for Mental Health Services," *Administration in Mental Health*, Fall 1973, pp. 12–26.

14. G. Rosenberg, "Data Gathering Systems in Research and Evaluation," *Journal of the National Association of Private Psychiatric Hospitals*, Vol. 8, No. 3, Fall 1976, pp. 31–34.

15. H.R. 3 Medicare, Medicaid Anti-fraud, procedures published in the Federal Register, Vol. 44, No. 16, January 23, 1979, p. 4741.

16. "A Reporting System for Hospital Social Work Directors," Chicago, Illinois, AHA, 1978.

17. B. Berkman, and H. Rehr, "Social Work Undertakes its Own Audit," *Social Work in Health Care*, Vol. 3, No. 3, Spring 1978, pp. 273–285.

18. Washington State Chapter Society of Hospital Social Work Directors, unpublished memo, October 1975.

19. Standards for Social Work Programs in Short-Stay Hospitals, New York City

Chapter NASW and Metropolitan New York Chapter of the Society of Hospital Social Work Directors, February 1977.

20. *Development of Professional Standards Review for Hospital Social Work,* American Hospital Association, Chicago, Ill., 1977.

21. Standards for Hospital Social Work Services, prepared by the Joint Committee of the American Hospital Association and the National Association of Social Workers, for presentation to the Joint Commission on Accreditation of Hospitals. Approved by the Board of Directors, NASW, October 1976.

5

The Chart Notation

ALMA T. YOUNG

Introduction

The medical record is the daily repository of critical information concerning the patient. That information is factual, historical, behavioral, conjectural, leading to diagnostic and therapeutic formulations. The patient's medical chart, which also serves as an historical document covering past findings for any future needs, is the only source for key material and, as such, is the medium of communication among those involved in caring for the patient in the health facility, each of whom has the responsibility for maintaining its accuracy, objectivity, and quality. The social worker in a health care setting, one of many professionals involved in the patient's care, enters the situation bringing a knowledge base geared to understanding of the patient's social needs, the patient and family's social functioning and lifestyle, cultural patterns, and the availability of community resources as related to the patient's physical condition. The social worker's ability to communicate with the other professionals caring for the patient is crucial to the treatment process, and frequently to the diagnostic, as well. The social worker's notations can influence the attitude and behavior of the other professionals, who share the overall goals but differ in viewpoint, and may ultimately affect the perception and behavior of the patient and family members.

In social work, medical chart recording has been accepted as one means of better communication with other professionals involved with the patient and family. When done well, it can be a most effective means of exchange. In the past, much time has been devoted to acquainting health care professionals and paraprofessionals with the contributions of social work to total patient care, typically through the single case discussion with physicians or in interprofessional "rounds." While still invaluable for its immediate on-the-spot exchange, this method, unfortunately, did not permit development of a structure whereby the social work contributions could be readily accessible and retrievable. The recorded statement is the major means by which all the health care professions can meet the purpose of professional accountability.

With the passage of P.L. 92-603, in 1972, establishing Professional Standards Review Organizations (PSROs), accountability, quality assurance, and similar terms began to take on new meaning for social workers. While the original legislation and policies were developed to review physician care, the law and the program manual clearly stated that, in time, non-physician health care practitioners will be involved in reviewing the care provided by their peers.[1] Even before the federal regulations concerning peer review, the Joint Commission on Accreditation of Hospitals (JCAH) Standards for Social Work Departments[2] and the New York State Department of Health Social Work Code[3] required that social work documentation be included in the patient's medical chart. (In 1972, under an annual review of hospital services, the New York State Department of Health found the Department of Social Work Services of The Mount Sinai Hospital in default of its requirement for chart documentation of services rendered; the Department was expected to correct this problem within two years, the time of the next review.) While these laws, regulations, and review did not alter *basic* social work practice, they did introduce a structure for documentation of the social work services provided. Thus, they provided the impetus and the mandate by which social work departments can examine the nature and the quality of practice as denoted in the medical chart.

The Setting

This chapter describes the process used by the Department of Social Work Services at The Mount Sinai Hospital to develop a social work chart notation system, to evaluate continuously its current system, and to devise a means to measure quality and quantity of services provided. The Department, like many others, had previously maintained its own social service records, in which detailed notes recorded at various intervals highlighted social work interventions over a period of time, and served as sources of information for future reference. In addition, brief social service notes were entered in the medical charts in order to maintain a system of communication with other professionals about psycho-social factors relating to the patient's medical condition. This method, while useful for periodic communication at critical stages during the course of the patient's care, was not problem-free; it suffered from communication lags and lack of continuity in day-to-day operation.

As the staff proceeded to implement the mandated regulations for chart notations, they remained aware of the fact that change would create problems among social workers and others involved in patient care. Sufficient documentation existed in the literature and in the staff's experience to show that the social service written entries were anything but consistent, or even uniform enough for evaluation purposes. Knowing that the recording of interventions had had very little professional development, the staff gave first consideration to how and what to write in a chart. Therefore, establishing a forum to provide the opportunity for input from all levels of the social work staff was critical in this initial phase. The immediate concerns at this stage were: (1) to translate "recording" into the medical chart into its value terms as a patient care document; (2) to make a smooth transition from social service separate record-keeping to an all-inclusive medical record; (3) to modify the present recording style in such a way that ultimately it could reflect the quality of service through the inclusion of clear, concise, and meaningful social-psychological material; and (4) to demonstrate that the record could serve as a means of professional accountability.

Development of Chart Notations Committee

After considering the size of the Department, of whom 65 staff members were trained MSWs in direct contact with patients and families, and the uniqueness of some service areas, a committee consisting of practitioners, supervisors, and administrators was established with representation from all service areas—medical/surgical, psychiatry, ambulatory care, obstetrics, pediatrics, and so on. The Committee began its work in the spring of 1972, and, as expected, initial reactions were mixed. As the rationale for change evolved, all the apprehensions about writing per se reappeared. Many were translated into specific problems: (1) developing a clear, concise style of recording, with critical assessment and prediction about a patient/family and less description; (2) utilizing written material with other disciplines, seemingly a less interactional means of dealing with critical social and emotional factors in illness; (3) fearing that the written inclusion of information shared with social workers might jeopardize the confidentiality commitment to patients; and (4) solving the existing problem of general access to and availability of medical charts. While the importance of these concerns could not be minimized, the Committee had to face the reality that change in the system was necessary. It became obvious that the immediate task was to channel anxieties into productive activities that would lead to rational solutions.

The Chart Notations Committee identified its immediate goals: (1) to establish a policy for chart notations in conformity with the requirements of the Joint Commission on Accreditation of Hospitals and the New York State Health Department, (2) to provide guidelines for content of chart notations, (3) to recommend a method for early implementation, and (4) to devise a means for monitoring chart entries. With an implementation target date of January 1973, the importance of the change became more of a reality. The Committee agreed that the goals outlined would concern the professional staff and would relate to recording for clinical practice, that any revisions in chart notations entered by social work assistants and social health advocates would be deferred until a later date. For the social work staff, a system whereby the supervisor co-signed chart entries already existed. (Recording for purposes of teaching and research were not to be considered; these would depend on the needs determined by the preceptor and research staff, but it was believed that the change would ultimately affect these areas also.) Scheduled weekly meetings were arranged to discuss, initially, each of the previously mentioned and new concerns, while Committee members moved into planning efforts.

Content of chart notes was one initial area for concentration. Each Committee member focused on the uniqueness of the service with which he or she was familiar, believing that the first commitment was to fellow workers, to defend the need for a particular format and style of recording. Confidentiality became a major theme, with the primary concern the misuse and misinterpretation of content by other personnel who had access to the charts. Discussion of this topic provoked a great deal of anxiety, and the desire to maintain only the traditional style of social service chart recording was pervasive. It was apparent that the confidentiality issue masked the significance of the exposure of professional content to "others," and the social workers' reluctance to enter their material into the more open medical chart. By design, this issue was never fully addressed. Instead, in considering the content of chart notes, attention was directed to two specific areas: (1) the purpose of the chart notes, and (2) the selection of critical data and information.

Purposes of Chart Notes and Selection of Content

The early discussion concerned the primary purposes of the medical record: to provide relevant daily information dealing with the diagnosis and the treatment given during the course of the patient's care; to serve as a means of communication among professionals involved in the patient's care and the historical record of the patient's illness or disability course in the Hospital.[4] Many health care practitioners are not always sufficiently aware of the use of record as medico-legal evidence in matters of insurance, court hearings, compensation, and the like. Furthermore, it was essential to emphasize the significance of the record as a primary tool, utilized by accreditation bodies such as the JCAH and by regulatory agencies of federal, state, and local health services.

The selection of material to be included in the medical chart is fundamental to the social worker's concept of relevancy. The first step in this process is clear understanding of the reason for involvement with the patient/family. This clarity of purpose is necessary regardless of the source of entry (referral, screening, or 100 percent coverage for high risk factors identified within a given setting). The worker must keep in mind that reason(s) for involvement may or may not be as stated in referral or in the initial contact with patient/family. Initial assessment of the patient's medical condition, socio-environmental situation, and emotional reactions is critical. Another step in the selection of content is identification of problem(s) for social work intervention(s). While many problems presented or uncovered during the assessment cannot, and perhaps should not, be dealt with immediately, problems relevant to the patient's medical care and planning should be documented, the priority being given to those jointly arrived at between social worker and the patient/family. Interventions made to solve the problems identified are pertinent to the total treatment plan, and should be annotated concisely. All too often, the tendency to record all information for future reference overshadows the immediate purpose for which the record is intended. The key to selecting content for chart notes is to limit information to that which is pertinent and meaningful rather than descriptive.

Development and Implementation of Guidelines

The Committee members recognized that this approach contrasted with the usual method of annotating charts, and took steps to develop basic guidelines for the content of chart notes. The Committee's experience of writing and reviewing sample notes in accordance with the tentative guidelines before releasing these for general implementation became the training method for other members of the Department.

All activities and discussion initiated in Committee meetings were brought into units* for deliberation. This feedback system provided valuable exchange of ideas and helped to maintain a broad perspective of problems and progress. While Committee members were able to resolve their own conflicts on specific issues in Committee meetings, they encountered similar and dissimilar problems when they returned to their units to present specific recommendations. In recognizing that the implementation of the new policy would require the involvement of all staff members, it was agreed that the structure for learning and the eventual monitoring of entries should take place in regularly scheduled unit meetings and in the overall supervisory system.

*A unit consists of a small cluster of staff in a specific service area, e.g., obstetrics, pediatrics.

The work already done by each Committee member in his or her own unit to prepare colleagues for the change had proved invaluable, as the Department moved to implement the policy on a trial basis in conjunction with its philosophy of testing before finalizing.

When the issue of monitoring entries was first introduced, the reactions were predictable. Staff members felt unqualified to monitor peers, and supervisors did not want to be put in the position of "breathing down staff back." The opportunity for discussion and freedom of expression in unit meetings helped to resolve some of these feelings. Both methods were eventually put into effect: staff began to review each other's cases within the units, and supervisors found the review of medical chart notes an additional and valuable tool in teaching beginning and new staff.

When the guidelines for chart notations were distributed, one characteristic that all agreed could not be tampered with was individual writing style. The design allowed for flexibility in writing style, service demands, and special forms used in some service areas. Frequency of recording specified minimum expectations and outlined general requirements for individual and group contacts. (See Exhibit 11.)

Follow-up: Problems and Progress

Three months after implementation, in January 1973, the Committee held a series of meetings to review problems and progress. The early consensus was that notations were being entered in the medical records and thus staff was meeting the requirement for accountability. Evidence that communication with other disciplines had increased appeared in comments from physicians and other professionals about social workers' activities, in more questions being raised regarding follow-up, and in requests for further information on specific patients.

Although there had been a well-organized plan for chart retrieval in order to deal with insertion of notes in outpatient charts, major problems occurred in securing the medical records, a difficulty also encountered by the clinics and other service departments. Confidentiality continued to be an area of concern to the social workers, now due less to the belief in possible abuse of content, and more to the professional struggle in determining what is pertinent to others involved in the patient's care. Helping staff learn to write their assessments and relevant content into chart notes continued to be a primary area for concentration. Such writing had always been a problem to social workers and continued to be. The unit structure remained the most direct means for continued learning and the agreed-upon approach for monitoring each other's entries.

Long-range planning included staff educational programs and seminars across service lines, with thought being given to the uniqueness of each service and the special problems each presented. The separate social service chart was totally discontinued. There is occasional need for a special and separate record, such as in child abuse situations or in transfers to other treatment facilities, which the Department retains for its accountability in addition to medical record entries.

The Final Stage and Implementation

The Chart Notations Committee was reactivated in the fall of 1974 with three major purposes: (1) to review the initial guidelines and determine how well they had been implemented throughout the Department; (2) to amend and/or revise the guidelines in the light of experience gained; and (3) to make specific recommendations for implementation of a peer review system. The Committee representation remained essentially the same with the exception that no supervisory staff joined (this was not by design).

Initial discussions revealed that chart notation had been an area of concern in all units since its inception; however, it had not received any priority in the units' discussions. Each unit was recognizably at a different stage in regard to quality, quantity, frequency, and monitoring of chart notes. The Committee quickly agreed on the need to establish a more structured system for ongoing unit-based discussions in order to help staff arrive at a more uniform method for chart notations and review.

A simple one-page form with questions relating to minimal expectations for chart notes was developed for review of entries in the units. (See Exhibit 12.) The questions were designed to elicit information on: (1) dates of entries, (2) frequency of chart notes, (3) reason for entry, (4) social worker's assessment, (5) definition of problem, (6) goals, and (7) description of interventions. The reviewers' impressions were thought to be vital in assessing the overall quality of the chart notes. Again, the Committee members assumed a leadership role in implementing this initial structured format in their respective units. Knowing that the previous recording style did not lend itself to specific answers to these seven questions, considerable leeway was granted by the reviewers during the initial period. More important, staff became consciously aware of the lack of clarity in the chart entries. The exposure of case material for review by others was not new to some of the more experienced staff members, since many of them had engaged in record reviews for other purposes. However, learning to record in a more structured manner held greater difficulty for them than for new staff who had not yet become attached to the traditional recording style. On the basis of experience within the units, the Committee recommended further testing of the chart review method for a limited period. Supervisors, at their own requests, were later included on the Committee, and their presence was not considered a deterrent to the leadership role assumed by the practicing staff; actually their presence helped to integrate objectives and implementation among all levels of staff.

The Department's administrative staff, allowing for extensions, held to a final implementation date of January 1976 for the system of chart review to be operational within the Department. The Chart Notations Committee was eager to cease its activity with a format that all had tested and found acceptable. It was felt that staff had demonstrated the need to engage more openly in discussions about recording and to improve practice as well as recording skills; therefore, the final stage of the Committee's activities was devoted to a more structured review method whereby each unit maintained its own record of charts reviewed, and of the reviewers. Comments and criticisms were emphasized since these dealt with information that was either unclear or had little meaning for the workers' purpose. Gradually a shift occurred from concern about "criticizing a colleague" to examining how practice was reflected in chart notes. In the knowledge that a chart review method by social workers had been mandated, the staff implemented one.

Summary

One key factor in this descriptive account of the Chart Notations Committee was the early involvement of staff in the process. The Committee structure of projecting ideas, testing them in small groups, and returning to the Committee for refinement allowed for staff-based enterprise. Despite the initial resistance to change, increased levels of anxiety when new steps were introduced, and natural peer protectiveness when the reality of a structured method seemed imminent, the Committee demonstrated a readiness to assume responsibility and to make the process a staff-based enterprise. With clear understanding of expectations, clear identification of learning needs, the Department of Social Work Services proceeded to formalize the next steps in the process. Concurrently, staff became involved in seminars dealing with specific areas of practice, development of a peer review committee, and restructuring of individual supervisory methods.

The original guidelines for recording and the form used for chart review served as a frame of reference in developing new tools for staff education programs. The recent guidelines are both descriptive and directive, giving special attention to the need for documenting information that is relevant as well as reasons for omitting information that is pertinent. (See Exhibit 13.) Questions on the one-page form were grouped into the following: (1) reason for entry, (2) assessment, (3) collaboration, (4) contract/goals, (5) intervention, and (6) outcome. When these had been translated into questions which they could ask of themselves, the staff seemed better able to grasp the content to be included.

1. Reason for entry—Why am I involved with patient/family?
2. Assessment—What is the problem(s) as seen by patient/family?
3. Collaboration—Who else is involved in the patient's care?
4. Contract/Goals—What did we (patient/family and worker) agree to work on in order of priority?
5. Intervention—What were my interventions in order to resolve or alleviate the problem(s)?
6. Outcome—What happened? Or where do we go from here?

If the above questions are to be answered appropriately, social workers will need: (1) to utilize their professional skills in assessing the specific problem(s) for which social work interventions are needed, (2) to collaborate effectively with other professionals involved in the patient's care, and (3) to record these contacts so that they relate to the assessment, diagnostic appraisal, and plans. Although brevity is a major concern, it should not be a reason for incompleteness. Information considered pertinent to the patient/family situation should be meaningful to others involved. The organization of content can help to sharpen the thinking process and help in the selection of information to be included in the chart note. Equally important is the fact that workers must remember that they are recording for people other than social workers and that not all of these are professionals.

Conclusions

The implementation of a structured method for chart notation and review is one step toward achievement of the long-range goal—written documentation that reflects quality practice. While there is still uncertainty as to whether quality of recording equals quality practice, "the profession of social work has an inherent responsibility for developing quality and quality assurances."[5] The opportunity for ongoing learning experiences to enhance practice and improve recording skills must be formalized and incorporated as part of a department's overall program if the ultimate goal is to be achieved.

References*

1. *Development of Professional Standards Review for Hospital Social Work,* Chicago, Illinois, American Hospital Association, 1977.

2. *Ibid.,* p. 4.

3. New York State Hospital Code, Chapter V (pertaining to social service departments in hospitals) 700, 2(d).

4. Mary Hemelt and Mary Mackert, "Factual Medical Records Protect Hospitals, Practitioners, Patients," *Journal of American Hospital Association,* Vol. 51, July 1, 1977, pp. 50–51.

*Harriett Bartlett, *Social Work Practice in the Health Field* (National Association of Social Workers, 1961) served as an overall reference source.

5. Helen Rehr, "Quality Assurance: Issues for Social Services in Health," in *Proceedings: Quality Assurance in Social Services in Health Programs for Mothers and Children,* edited by William T. Hall and Gerald St. Denis, Pittsburgh, Pennsylvania, April 1975, pp. 35–53. The Institute was planned and implemented by the Joint Public Health-Social Work Training Project MCH #114 and with financial support from the Bureau of Community Health Services, HEW Contract # HSA-105-74-83.

6

Developing a Peer Review System

ROSLYN H. CHERNESKY
AND ALMA T. YOUNG

Peer review is a method for evaluating the quality of care given by an individual practitioner and the quality of care provided to patients by a health institution—in this instance, the Department of Social Work Services. As an evaluation method, it differs from and complements other approaches that are helpful in assessing the effectiveness and efficiency of services provided. Characteristics of a peer review system include: (1) determination of professionally recognized standards of care for acceptable and non-acceptable behavior against which performance and service are compared, (2) an ongoing and systematic process by which practicing professionals monitor the quality of care given by their colleagues as demonstrated in their chart notations (medical audit) to determine whether practice is in accordance with the designated standards and criteria, (3) compilation of review results to identify patterns of trends in the quality of service provided (social health care evaluations), and (4) establishment of corrective mechanisms to deal with deficiencies identified as related to individual performance and to organizational or system problems.

The Department of Social Work Services of The Mount Sinai Hospital established a Peer Review Committee of twelve social workers to review a sample of their colleagues' charts every week. Impetus for the peer review system came from at least three sources: (1) the Department's concern with assuring that it is providing social work services of a high quality; (2) the social work profession's desire to respond to the growing demand that it justify the effectiveness, the need, and the efficiency of its work; and (3) recent federal legislation mandating the establishment of professional standards review organizations (PSROs).

A retrospective look at the Department's experience in developing its peer review system makes it possible to identify what may have been some of the critical factors that contributed to its success in establishing the system. After three and one-half years with the Chart Notations Committee, and one year devoted directly to developing a peer review system, the system is in full operation. The system is far from perfect; it is not yet clear whether the results are worth the investment or whether the same results might be attained with a less expensive procedure. Changes are continuously being made, and the system is subject to a full evaluation. Nevertheless, it is now possible to share what the authors believe are the advantages and disadvantages of the model developed and which account for the Department's progress.

This chapter will describe the process used to develop the Mount Sinai peer review system and focus upon those factors, decisions, and steps that appear to have been critical to its establishment.

Structure

Drawing upon the experience and success of the Chart Notations Committee, a similar structure and process were used to develop a peer review system. The similarities consisted of: (a) the use of a staff committee with delegated responsibility for planning the system's design and implementation; (b) the leadership of a social work department administrator working closely with the committee, providing direction and support, setting goals, time limits, and facilitating the committee's work; (c) an expectation of and procedure for regular feedback from all staff; and (d) continual revisions and changes responsive to concerns and needs of all staff. The major difference between the structural arrangement for developing the peer review system and the work of the Chart Notations Committee was use of a consultant.

This consultant, who had not previously been affiliated with the Hospital or the Department, worked directly with the assistant director and indirectly with the Peer Review Committee, introducing into the planning process some expertise and experience which could be drawn upon as needed or desired. The consultant met regularly with the assistant director to prepare for the committee meetings and to assess problems and/or progress. She designed the instruments and prepared initial drafts of the necessary material, allowing the assistant director to respond and to revise rather than to develop materials from the beginning. Together, the process was planned and examined; however, as is appropriate in a consultant-client relationship, the decision to follow up on suggestions or to use any of the materials was left to the assistant director. During the first six months, the Peer Review Committee met weekly with the assistant director and consultant to: (1) design the instrument to be used for peer review, (2) consider some of the problems related to developing the system, and (3) prepare members as well as their colleagues for peer review. Although it was perhaps unnecessary for the consultant to attend each meeting, the disadvantages of sporadic attendance to the group's development and to the entire process were considered to be too great.

The administrator who chaired the Committee was especially attuned to the phases of the Committee's development and to the need for group maintenance as well as task achievements. Whether a staff member not at an administrative level might have performed the same role, is a question of interest. A very specific function of this administrator was to link administration with the Committee's activities, and to share with the Committee the administrative responses to its work as well as to the priorities.

Dealing with the Assumptions
of Peer Review

During the first few months, the Peer Review Committee dealt with the assumptions upon which peer review is based. The major assumptions were critically examined, although it was recognized that, as assumptions, any one of them could prove invalid.

Beginning with the premise that good social work practice is substantially different from bad, the Committee assumed that social workers know and can recognize the difference. Admission and acceptance of this premise came more easily when peer review was seen as a way to formalize what has been an informal system among social workers in a department or agency: if asked which of your colleagues you would want to provide social work services for a relative entering the hospital, staff can admit there are indeed differences among social work practitioners—which imply that some are better and others worse. Identifying characteristics or qualities of practice that lead to that kind of judgment brought the Committee to a discussion of criteria of good social work practice and further confirmed that, in fact, the Committee was only formalizing what was already informally known.

A second assumption the Committee addressed was that chart notations can serve as an indicator of good and bad social work practice. The belief that quality of recording reflected quality of performance was a much harder assumption for staff to accept; introducing the limited empirical data in support of this premise is seldom convincing.[1] Staff may eventually acknowledge that a poor practitioner, who has not adequately identified the appropriate problems or points of intervention, would be unlikely to demonstrate in his recording that he has rendered good service regardless of how well he writes or how fully developed his notes. Generally, staff, at this initial stage, are unlikely to believe that a good piece of practice is frequently recorded in a way that demonstrates the quality of work. Only as staff themselves see the evidence, by examining chart notations, do they come to accept this assumption.

The third assumption was that workers can monitor and evaluate the work of their colleagues.[2] Although this assumption rests on a prior one, that social workers should monitor and evaluate colleagues' practice, this Committee had no need to deal with it. Prior activities with chart notations made this staff aware of the role and responsibility of professionals to assure quality service. Elsewhere this may not be so, and therefore the situation will need to be handled differently.

The Committee did not question if they should evaluate peers but whether they could objectively and critically examine their colleagues' work and pass judgment on it.[3] They were undoubtedly somewhat surprised to find how easy, rather than how difficult, it was to do so. If anything, initial reviews tended to be more harsh than gentle, perhaps overly critical, with too demanding a level of expectation. Recognition of the need for some guidelines or criteria upon which to base evaluations, to direct and temper judgments, and to inject some objectivity emerged from this experience.

A fourth and final assumption concerned the value of a peer review. Implicit in the federal mandate to establish professional review systems, in NASW's support for social work participation in them, and in the enthusiasm with which departments—including the Mount Sinai Department of Social Work Services—have begun to implement such programs, was the assumption that professional review is sufficiently valuable to warrant the investment of departmental resources that implementation requires. Whether professional review is worthwhile can only be demonstrated through experience. By the careful selection of initial charts for peer review, the Committee can see incidents or situations which, if found in a number of cases, could be viewed as serious in terms of the quality of care received by patients. Although it is premature to conclude that a major problem exists with the examination of *one* case which highlights a questionable situation, the peer review system provides valuable indicators of possible areas for change or problems for resolution.

Designing the Review Instrument

The Committee's first task in developing the peer review system was to review the one-page form previously used by staff in working with the Chart Notations Committee. The instrument was expanded to include a tentative form covering five areas which were presented to the Committee at their first meeting with the consultant. These areas were: (1) recording of chart notations, (2) reason for initial contact, (3) assessment, (4) contract, and (5) social work intervention.

In order to prepare a useful instrument, the Committee immediately engaged in the practice reviews; from a master list of closed social service cases, several were selected each week for Committee review. Closed cases were decided upon because of a number of advantages: (1) they were more easily accessible, (2) they demonstrated a completed process by the worker, (3) they eliminated the need to involve staff in record selection, and (4) they obviated the need for on-site review (inpatient charts). The records used were selected because of their illustrative value.

During the first months of practice, social work notations were copied from the records and presented without worker identification but with the abstracts of relevant medical problem and management.[4] The record was not, however, disguised.

Using the initial instrument, each question was read aloud and the twelve members agreed on an answer. The deliberations required to reach consensus pointed out limitations of the questions (meaning, wording, response, categories, redundancy, too few or too many questions) and differences in understanding and interpretation of chart notes. Although many questions were dropped, the overall effect of the refinement was to get at the concept of quality service through a fuller range of dimensions and criteria. The current form, which is the fourth revision, relates to five areas: (1) reason for entry, (2) assessment, (3) contract/ goals, (4) intervention, and (5) collaboration. (See Exhibit 14.)

The Committee found that the more precise the questions on the review form, the easier it was to judge the quality of practice. There was a point at which, however, too explicit questions would affect the judgment by rendering it almost impossible to answer. The tendency in answering questions was to avoid "Yes" or "No" whenever possible and to respond in terms of a third category— Don't know, Not sure, Not applicable. Therefore third response categories were deliberately eliminated in the design of the instrument and were phased in gradually, when necessary.

Two kinds of questions were developed: factual and evaluative. The first allow only for a response of "Yes" or "No." For example, is the date of initial contact noted? Evaluative questions require professional judgment in order to answer them; rarely can they be answered with a simple "Yes" or "No." These items ask about adequacy and appropriateness and, because of their complexity, can be answered only by individuals with the same professional training and experience—peers.[5]

One would anticipate in the long run greater agreement in responses to factual questions than to evaluative questions. In the beginning, however, there is not necessarily greater consistency in answers to the factual questions because of the tendency to answer factual questions and judgmental questions in the same way. Beginning reviewers are apt to "read into" the chart notations, to give the benefit of the doubt, and to avoid answering "No."

More important, perhaps, is the fact that initially the recording guidelines were insufficiently precise, and workers therefore differed considerably in how they recorded seemingly direct items of information. As the guidelines were refined and used by staff for their records, reviewers could answer factual questions in closer agreement.

One valuable aspect of the review instrument is the opportunity for the review team to comment, summarizing its evaluation of the practice as recorded. Comments are the key to the educational component of the peer review system. To be helpful, comments must be critical and objective, acknowledging good as well as bad practice, and providing some indication of how practice can be improved. The Committee learned how to comment incisively and with insight. Members quickly developed an approach that made their comments supportive and helpful, and balanced the delicacy of peer evaluations against the need for accountability and for quality care. Probably the participation of supervisors in the teams contributed to the team's ability to adapt to this aspect of the review so easily. A few months after the committee had practiced with the review form the writing of comments was introduced and, at the same time, the need for an overall quality rating was suggested.

The Committee considered such a rating necessary to provide a relatively simplified summary of the quality of performance practice in each dimension; an overall rating would be useful to the individual practitioner and for compilation of a Department profile. The Committee selected the terms—excellent, good, fair, poor—which were thought to be most descriptive and least offensive. Completing this aspect of the review apparently offered the most difficulty to the reviewers. The summary rating clearly exceeded a total of the "Yes" and "No" answers in each quality dimension, and reviewers did not rate on that basis. Nevertheless, they recognized that a relationship existed between the two and that the summary rating had to be consistent with the other responses and with the comments. No doubt the basis for the rating was never made sufficiently clear, and reviewers were therefore left with considerable discretion for judgment. The uneasiness of this situation, along with the real difficulty in categorizing and labeling quality performance, contributed to this less-than-optimal aspect of the review. Some indication appeared that staff members, upon receiving their completed reviews, were reacting to the summary ratings rather than to the comments or the total instrument: the ratings assumed more significance than was either intended or warranted. While such staff response may not be surprising, it was unanticipated and thought to be dysfunctional. Although the Committee considered eliminating the summary rating from the review, it decided not to do so until the value of a summary rating component was clearer.

The Peer Review Committee found numbers of charts with only one social service note which did not lend themselves to the current review procedure. This discovery led to the design of an additional review form for single note entry, one which, contrary to the other instrument, asks only seven questions that focus on reason for involvement, interventions, and disposition. The single entry form was designed for review of those cases in which the totality of social work intervention and disposition were recorded in only one chart notation; it was not to be used when incomplete recording resulted in only one notation. The form has been most useful on services such as emergency room contact and abortion service where the need for social work interventions may be brief or even a one-time contact. (See Exhibit 15.)

Educating Colleagues

As the Committee designed the review instrument, and met weekly to practice review of records, members became increasingly aware of the experience's effect on the quality of their own practice and recording and that their colleagues lacked the advantages of the Committee experience and would, therefore, be less likely to demonstrate equally good practice and recording of practice. The Committee felt it was essential to prepare all staff for peer review; each Committee member took responsibility for presenting to her staff unit the drafts of the review form, encouraging use of these as a guide to social work recordings, and practicing reviews of records. Each unit progressed at its own pace, convening often and devoting as much time as desired to peer review. By the time of a departmental staff meeting devoted to a discussion of peer review, nearly all staff were already familiar with it. They had actually worked with the instrument, had had the opportunity to react to the form and the process, and knew that their comments had been relayed to the Peer Review Committee for probable action.

The reaction and the experience of the unit members to the developing system were an important aspect of the Committee's work. Although specific changes were seldom requested, the negative and positive feelings of staff were valuable clues that influenced the progress of the Committee.

Placing responsibility for educating colleagues and for receiving feedback upon Committee members was more than a pragmatic approach to reach all staff. Committee members became more fully involved in the development of the peer review system. Having to explain, teach, and convey to colleagues what peer review was and how it would operate required active Committee participation and led to greater staff investment in the system and its effectiveness.

This role and responsibility of Committee members increased during the period of the system's development, complemented by other departmental changes that reinforced the development of the self-regulated practitioner, a redefinition of the role of preceptors and the function of staff development programs.

Learning to Engage in Peer Review

During the six-month period in which the Committee designed the instruments, educated their colleagues, and practiced reviewing charts, a number of changes in the Committee members and their functioning as peer reviewers became noticeable. Most obvious was the Committee's growing sophistication, reflected in recordings.

The Committee members began to see the entire picture of social work input as related to total patient care, as well as the need for and extent of social work involvement with the patient and family. Discussions on cases and on the quality of social work practice became more meaningful and more objective in terms of workers' performance. The Committee was better able to identify more clearly specific areas in which poor or good quality was likely to emerge in relation to reason for entry, assessment, contract, interventions, and collaboration. Inadequate performance in just one of these areas was likely to be an indicator of poor quality of service. Good service seldom occurred if, for example, the worker did not really understand why she was involved, what were the patient's medical and social problems, and the priorities for dealing with the patient/family at that time, and if her professional interventions did not include interdisciplinary collaboration or activities consistent with the contract/goals. When the practice reviews began, it was not often possible to get this information from the social service notes. Social workers' recordings tended to be skimpy and not necessarily focused so as to enable reviewers to judge performance in each of these critical areas. As recordings improved and social work practice revealed in recording improved, it became considerably easier to review charts.

Initially the Committee thought the fault of most problems was external to the individual worker and symptomatic of a procedure for a particular service area. Gradually, the essence of good social work performance which transcends the uniqueness of worker style, service requirements, or system became the subject of quality assessment. By the time the Committee members were assessing quality of performance in terms of these essential components of practice and service (which were then incorporated into a revised draft of the review instrument), they were less likely to attribute the majority of the problems found to the institution.

The growth and development of the Committee members coincided with the move to a more realistic peer review format, one that was similar to the actual procedure to be used for peer review. Whereas the Committee had begun practicing reviews using unidentified chart abstracts, the total chart was eventually substituted for abstracts. This was most helpful for the reviewers, because it allowed the social service notes to be seen in the full context of the medical condition, course of treatment, and interventions by all disciplines. Although it was no longer possible to review charts anonymously, knowledge of the individual worker appeared to have no real effect upon the way the review was conducted.[6] None of the Committee members' own charts were selected for these practice reviews, and an attempt was made to avoid the use of charts of Committee members' supervisors or supervisees. When a supervisee's chart was used inadvertently, the member who was the worker's supervisor did not inform the Committee and appeared outwardly unaffected. Later, the supervisor could reveal how difficult the experience had been, especially if the worker received a poor rating which could not be defended or accounted for and for which, consequently, the supervisor felt reflected upon her ability.

Method of Peer Review

The Committee began practicing reviews as a whole but eventually the total of twelve was divided into teams of three. At this stage there was no attempt to designate the teams purposefully. However, no more than one supervisor was supposed to be on each team nor was any team to be composed of staff from only one service. Mixing and matching of members was encouraged, to allow wider opportunity to serve with one another and in all possible combinations, partly to see if particular staff combinations seemed dysfunctional. The possibility existed that some staff would be less or more active and willing to assert their points of view and judgment with some colleagues rather than others, although in fact this did not happen.

Each team was given charts to review; these independent reviews took place simultaneously in the four corners of the room. When the team model was first tried, at least one chart was reviewed by more than one team in order to allow comparison of results and verify for everyone the existence of a common understanding and consensus on quality rating. Although every question within each quality dimension did not necessarily receive the same response from more than one team, the general team evaluations as evidenced in the overall rating and comments were so similar that they created considerable confidence in the peer review process being used.[7]

Finalizing Preparation for Implementation

After six months of planning, preparation, and practice, the review instrument, although still in a draft stage, was nearly final. Fewer and fewer changes were made in the items or response categories. The Committee had acquired skill, comfort, and facility through the practice of reviews; the social work staff had become familiar with peer review and the expectations for their recordings and social work practice. In addition to the unit and staff meetings and the staff development seminars used as a forum for discussion of peer review, guidelines for recording (Exhibit 13), the review instruments and a manual describing the Department's peer review system had been distributed to all staff. The manual confirmed in writing some of the rules and procedures that staff had been told of and also introduced, for the first time, several new areas that dealt with rights and responsibilities of staff, administration, and the Peer Review Committee.

July and August of 1976 were used to finalize preparation for implementation. During this time, the Committee of twelve was divided into permanent teams of three and reviewed, in teams, on a regularly scheduled basis. This was a trial period, used to iron out any last-minute problems or unanticipated consequences. The procedures for retrieving medical charts on an ongoing basis and for assigning charts to teams were finalized. The teams operated as if the system were already implemented; however, the results of their reviews were not returned to staff.

During this period other major decisions about implementation were made. In order to be consistent with the function of peer review and the development of self-regulated professionals, it was decided that only the worker would receive the results. Only supervisors and administrative staff were permitted to view the results in the administrative file. Although it is expected that the worker will turn to any of a number of supports provided by the Department, including the supervisor, better to understand the reason for the review rating and how this might be improved, it was thought appropriate that questions and complaints about the review process and system should be directed to those implementing it.

Mid-September saw formal implementation of the peer review system: (a) each review team met weekly, independent of the others, and reviewed two to four charts in a two-hour session; (b) a routine for selecting, retrieving, distributing, and returning charts was in operation; (c) a system for keeping track of individuals and service areas screened and reviewed had been set up; and (d) a mechanism for disseminating the review results to staff was in process.

The Professional Review (PR) System

The PR system in operation is best understood when portrayed in its four stages:

Chart Retrieval

1. From a master file of cases closed during the month, a random selection of cases are listed for each MSW.

Stage I

2. Charts are requested from medical records for screening.

Screening

1. Charts are examined to determine if they meet criteria for review. (See Exhibit 16.)
2. If appropriate for review, chart is assigned to one of four PR teams.

Stage II

3. If inappropriate for review, the reason for rejection is recorded.
4. Data maintained on (a) the charts that are reviewed and rejected for review, (b) which teams review each chart, (c) the number of reviews and screenings of each worker.

Review

1. Each PR team convenes once a week for a two-hour session and reviews 2 to 4 records.

Stage III

2. Charts and the completed review instruments are returned.

Monitoring and Feedback

1. Completed review instruments are duplicated.
2. Original is sent directly to worker reviewed; copy is kept in Department.

Stage IV

3. Responses to reviews received from workers where relevant.

4. Reviews are monitored for problems related to chart retrieval, screening, and review.

Evaluating the Peer Review System

Built into much of the system's implementation is a monitoring and feedback system that identifies problem areas and provides indicators of potential problems. Constant access to such information is critical for continuous upgrading and improvement of the system's operation. Changes are thus made continually as a result of new insight and information.

For example, as reviews became more sophisticated, it became apparent that the review form did not do justice to the quality dimension of outcome. Therefore new questions were added and the review form was again revised. When the Committee realized that a large number of records with only one social service notation were being screened out of the review process because they could not be adequately reviewed by teams with the original review form, a second form, for such charts only, was designed and tested. The Department had intended to establish a Peer Review Advisory Group, including representatives from staff, administration, and the Peer Review Committee, with responsibility for evaluating the system, making recommendations regarding changes in procedure, and addressing any problems that may arise. Because this has not yet been done, the responsibility and function of monitoring and feedback rests with the assistant director.

There are at least two other aspects of evaluation which, the Department recognizes need to be addressed. The first type of evaluation leads to mandated social health care evaluations, based upon the compilation of peer review results of individual workers and presenting a profile of overall quality of the Department's service and its progress toward attaining a high level of quality of service.

A second type of evaluation attempts to answer a more fundamental question of whether the peer review system that has been implemented is worthwhile. In order to answer this question, the benefits of the system in light of the costs must be examined and an attempt made to determine if the same results could be achieved through a more effective and less expensive system.

Having had the peer review system in operation for nine months, the Department has begun to examine and evaluate the system from a number of perspectives. Although the peer review system today is not exactly the same as the one initiated in September, the differences are relatively minor and reflect its adaptability and flexibility. The intent of the examination is to determine whether the system is as useful as anticipated and whether it is achieving its purpose: assuring the provision of a high quality of social work services. Available data on the quantity and quality of the reviews are being studied; general staff reaction to the peer review system will be incorporated. Completion of this evaluation with a recommendation on continuation and on changes that would make the system more effective and efficient represents the next, forthcoming stage of the Department's peer review system.

Conclusion

Although the formal evaluation of the peer review system is not yet complete, and it is premature to anticipate whether the results will support continuation of the system, it is possible to draw some conclusions from our experience with peer review in general and the Department's system in particular.

Those who have been intimately involved with the peer review system, especially the Committee members, have found their experience exciting and rewarding. Participation has brought to many a new opportunity for learning and professional development through and with colleagues. Committee members noticed almost immediately the impact of the review experience upon their own recording and practice. And, as they increasingly assumed the role of teacher within their units, they became further involved with and committed to the peer review process. In many ways, the greatest value of the system has been its impact on the Committee participants. With this in mind, efforts are under way gradually to introduce other staff to the teams, so that a sizeable number can experience the process.

There are indications that non-committee members have

also derived some benefit from the system. Staff, in general, seem to be clearer about their social work function, more focused with clients from the start, and more able to assess their practice for themselves. The Department has made use of the audit instruments on a regular basis in unit meetings, staff development seminars, and as part of orientation and supervision of new workers. This aspect of the system has permeated the Department. There is still, however, some strain felt by staff about quantity of recording; not all have clearly differentiated quality from quantity recording, and some staff still question all the criteria being used. For example, the need for evidence of social work collaboration with medical personnel is not uniformly accepted. There is no doubt that a minority continue to believe the system is a burden, that expectations are too unrealistic, and that it can be neither fair nor objective.

The enthusiasm of Committee members has often been dampened by the realities of practice demands. The time devoted to the peer review responsibilities must be made up by the worker in some way. Institutional supports to help workers resolve the conflict created by the peer review assignment and direct practice have not yet been established.

The realities of practice, especially the ever-increasing client population and the ever-decreasing staff complement, often intruded upon the Committee's work. The need to raise standards and to improve the quality of practice was upheld despite departmental retrenchment but with much difficulty. In part, in deference to this situation, it was decided that the teams would meet less often; that is, every other week. Reduction of teams from three to two members had been considered as an additional efficiency device, but, because Committee members opposed the notion, the idea was dropped.

The system developed at Mount Sinai appears to be somewhat expensive. Considerable time had to be taken for the Committee to prepare itself to begin review, during which the total social work staff became familiar with the recording and review expectations. The ongoing system uses a good deal of staff time as well as the time of the administrator and of those who assist in record retrieval and screening. Ideas on how to reduce costs and make the system more efficient have been explored, but all would have the effect of changing the nature of the system established (e.g., two-member rather than three-member teams, individual review rather than team review, monthly rather than weekly review).

The peer system can be influential in the development of other departmental activities. For example: (1) greater attention was given to the improvement of recording at regular unit meetings, (2) seminars were held in order to improve the quality of chart notations, and (3) staff development seminars were designed to help staff examine the quality of practice.

Maintaining the system's operation requires continuous staff input to monitor selection of staff to be reviewed, allocation of records to teams, return of audit forms to staff, and response to staff inquiries and complaints. Moreover, if each idea on how to reform the system, check its validity and reliability, and evaluate its effectiveness and efficiency were to be carried out, the departmental effort and costs would be even greater.

Without the evaluative data before us, aware of the need and desire to justify a peer review system, the authors can only declare at this time their strong belief that the overall impact of a peer review system on the staff and the Department has been positive—a rich experience that has indeed influenced the way workers are performing as well as recording.

References

1. The positive correlation between quality of recording and quality of performance was first found in a 1957 study of medical care in hospitals. Other studies have again indicated that measures of good recording performance and good care performance are related. As Donabedian stated, "Good recording is likely to be associated with good care mainly because the conditions that bring about good care are also responsible for bringing about good recording." See A. Donabedian, *A Guide to Medical Care Administration, Vol II: Medical Care Appraisal,* New York, APHA, 1969; T.F. Lyons, and B.C. Payne, "The Relationship of Physician Recording Performance to Their Medical Care Performance," *Medical Care* 12 (5): 463–469, 1974, and 12 (8): 714–720, 1974; L.S. Rosenfeld, "Quality of Medical Care in Hospitals," *AJPH* 47: 856–865, 1975.

2. Chernesky found in her study of social workers' attitudes toward participation in professional review that social workers will take on the responsibility for monitoring and evaluating colleagues although they do not especially like it or believe professional review is fair. See R. Chernesky, *A Training Program to Prepare Social Workers for Professional Review,* Unpublished DSW dissertation, CUNY, 1976.

3. Doubt about the validity and reliability of peer judgments has been expressed. Recent attempts to evaluate the quality of health care using peer review have led some to conclude that peer judgments are neither sufficiently accurate, nor homogenous enough to be of practical use. Other studies demonstrated that peer review could be improved. See, for example, R.H. Brook, and F.A. Appel, "Quality of Case Assessment: Choosing A Method for Peer Review," *New Eng. J. Med.* 288 (25): 1323–1329, 1973; F.M. Richardson, "Methodological Development of A System of Medical Audit," *Medical Care* 10 (6): 451–462, 1972; F.M. Richardson, "Peer Review of Medical Care," *Medical Care* 10 (1): 29–39, 1972.

4. Although we did not seriously consider using record abstracts, abstracted digests of records have been used for review. See R.H. Brook, and F.A. Appel, "Quality of Care Assessment: Choosing A Method for Peer Review," *New Eng. J. Med.* 288 (25): 1323–1329, 1973.

5. Our experience with the format of questions and the use of factual and evaluative questions parallels experience with the use of explicit and implicit criteria. Explicit criteria are characterized by predetermined and formal specification of standards to be used in the assessment which direct or instruct the reviewer to those aspects of care or practice that should be taken into consideration. Implicit criteria, on the other hand, leave the judgment to the reviewer and to his understanding of what is good or poor. The reviewer compares and judges the care provided as though it were his own. In effect, the reviewer is being asked whether he would have diagnosed and treated this particular patient in this particular manner under this particular circumstance. For a fuller discussion of standards and criteria see A. Donabedian, "Evaluating the Quality of Medical Care," *Milbank Memorial Fund Quarterly* 44: 166–203, 1966; and S.H. Kase, "Quality of Care Assessment," *PSRO: Organization for Regional Peer Review*, edited by B. Decker and P. Bonner, Cambridge, Mass.: Ballinger, 1973, pp. 174–190.

6. One study attempts to examine the potential impact of reviewer bias on judgments. Some bias, although not considered serious, was found in physicians' reviews where hospital identity was known. See D.W. Helbig, et al., "The Care Component Score—A New System for Evaluating Quality of Inpatient Care," *AJPH* 62: 540–546, 1972.

7. Higher agreement among reviewer ratings has been found when reviewers are trained and when teams or committees have the opportunity to work out differences of opinion and to discuss reasons for ratings. See, for example, D.F. Hinz, "Direct Observations as a Means of Teaching and Evaluating Clinical Skills," *J. Med. Educ.* 41: 150–161, 1966; J. Fine, and M.A. Morehead, "Study of Peer Review of In-Hospital Patient Care," *N.Y. State J. Med.* 71: 1963–1973, 1971; M.C. Phaneuf, *The Nursing Audit: Profile for Excellence*, New York, Appleton-Century Crofts, 1972.

7

Patient Care Evaluations (Audits):
Social Work Prerequisites
and Current Approaches

HELEN REHR
AND BARBARA BERKMAN

For a long time the service professions have planned to evaluate their practice. Many have been working on different methodologies to test a range of concerns. The publication *Evaluation* which terms itself "A Forum for Human Service Decision-Makers"[1] has included a veritable outpouring of program and practice (service) evaluations over the last six or seven years. Long before these somewhat sophisticated assessments appeared, a variety of reviewing mechanisms had been part of the hospital health care system. These assessments have been expected in most medical care institutions. Evaluations dealing with such areas as mortality review, tissue or pathology review, surgical review, ambulatory care review, and, most recently, medical audits of the delivery of care have been undertaken. Except for medical audits, these review structures are intended to discover questionable situations, occurring as a result of an individual practitioner's care, and are essentially performed by peer review. The Joint Commission on Accreditation (JCAH), the American Hospital Association (AHA), and the American Association of Medical Colleges (AAMC) regard such review mechanisms as one standard for accreditation. In spite of these institutional standard-setting methods, the federal government has imposed its own regulations, clearly indicating that institutional assessment has failed "to promote effective, efficient and economic delivery of proper quality. . . ."

Beginning in 1972, a range of quality and quantity controls on professional and institutional services have been mandated by federal regulations as a condition of reimbursement for care given. One aspect of the regulations is the Professional Standards Review Organization promulgated under P.L. 92–603, the Social Security Amendments. The medical care evaluation component of the PSRO legislation has been perceived as the "key" to improving delivery of inpatient services and, in the final analysis, to the continuing enhancement of the quality of patient care. In essence MCEs are expected to be patient care evaluations undertaken by the hospital. The evaluations are to be performed via professionally determined criteria or procedures, and by the professions themselves (peer review) as suggested by:

medical care criteria are predetermined elements against which aspects of the quality of a medical service may be compared. They are developed by professionals relying on professional expertise and on the professional literature.[2]

However, it is well understood that the evaluation of care itself does not necessarily result in improvement of practice. The PSRO regulation has recognized this and mandates that the results of measurement of care must be followed by action to correct what has been identified as problematic and that change will be evidenced. This change is to be tested in a follow-up study to demonstrate that improvement in patient care has indeed occurred. Thus, the MCE is followed by a feedback loop, which shares the findings and recommendations with the appropriate sector, and expects that recommendations will be implemented through whatever means are deemed valid. Where continuing education of practitioners is indicated, evidence will be needed to demonstrate that a training program of relevant content has been implemented.

While the language of the PSRO regulations refers to medical care evaluation, the approach has not been limited to care delivered by physicians. Non-physician health care practitioners contribute to patient care. A section in the PSRO Program Manual stipulates the involvement of non-physician health care practitioners in review.[3] The manual outlines the means by which non-physician health care practitioners shall review their performance and practice; the method is comparable to that of physicians, calling for professionally determined criteria, norms, and standards, with the assessment to be done by non-physician health care practice peers. Where care is jointly undertaken, an interdisciplinary assessment is expected. Where it is exclusively performed by non-physicians, then review will be done by that group. In any event the findings will be "reported through mechanisms established for review decisions related to physician care."[4]

In developing a quality assurance program for social work services in a hospital, the issue of whether to follow an interdisciplinary or solely a social work service method must be settled first. The likelihood of solo social work practice in a health care setting is remote, although not impossible, in view of the development of social therapy programs for certain kinds of distress and stress manifestations. The issue has been highlighted by Lurie with his expectation that social work programs in hospitals can follow both pathways. He encourages the development of professional criteria, permitting in its own measurable terms objective evaluation along prescribed determinants of process or patient care management. These he expects to undergo departmentally structured peer review, integrated into an interdisciplinary program of review. While Lurie cites the validity in the independence of professional peer review, he also notes "the interdependence of the disciplines" in the health care field. In addition, he calls attention to the many values in the sharing process which is a component of the institutional review system.[5]

A number of social work reviewing mechanisms have followed the route of "major diagnosis" and relevant social work practice. Social work audits have consequently developed along the lines of the illness-specific.[6] The belief underlying this method is that it can fit readily into medical care evaluations, which to date have been largely disease-specific. Other writers have concentrated audits in social problem and social stress terms.[7] This has been based on two premises: (1) social work has its own framework for identification of patient and family social needs irrespective of the disease-specific; and (2) it is possible to link social problems to any illness-specific, as social work integrates its own evaluative reviews into the interdisciplinary audit system. This approach supports independent social work audits, addressing the profession's own change of practice needs, while permitting such reviews to become a component of interdisciplinary patient care evaluations.

The Social Health Care Evaluation (SHCE), a Mount Sinai Department of Social Work Services audit, is conceptualized as a social work component of patient care evaluation, an evaluative study which should allow for a review of questions, concerns, and issues reflecting the quality of social work services given to patients. It is designed specifically to review factors related to the purpose and objectives of a hospital social work program. The major expectation of this evaluative review, with respect to professional performance, is that it uncover problems warranting change in the delivery of care. The review's findings and recommendations should result in essential changes, which in turn should facilitate the improvement of services. Feedback to the professional staff is another inherent expectation of the system, one which should also contribute to the resolution of continuing staff development needs uncovered by the review. This type of departmental review does not conflict with nor deny the importance of social work participation in *inter* or multidisciplinary patient care audits, and when further refined, SHCE should become a component in interdisciplinary reviews. At this time, social work should be an active member of institutional audit committees, bringing its own reviews and/or participating in interdisciplinary efforts.

In order for this type of review to become an integral, ongoing part of a department's service system, rather than merely a one-time study, the following prerequisites are necessary: (1) a reliable and valid continuous system of data collection; (2) a means of retrieving these data; and (3) the development and utilization of established norms, criteria, and standards to which review data can be compared. Once these prerequisites are achieved, the audit of social work services is feasible at any desired point in time. It is possible that reviews may ultimately be performed by trained personnel outside the social work system itself.

Most professional service systems have three interdependent components which may be reviewed for audit purposes: structural components of service, processes of service, and outcome of service. This chapter will elaborate on the prerequisites deemed necessary for implementation of any type of institutionalized review system and on the problems in current review approaches. In addition, The Mount Sinai Hospital's approach to social health care evaluation will be discussed.

Reliable and Valid Data Retrieval

The primary purpose of the medical record is to document care in the hospital. In this context, the record may be viewed as a means of ascertaining that health care practice and goals have been attained. Any medical record system should facilitate and demonstrate the achievement of health care objectives by all professionals who make entries in that system. Unfortunately medical recording is not standardized for uniform entry and records are frequently difficult to find, with data poorly organized and uneven in quality of entry—one basic obstacle to the retrieval of valid data in the medical setting. Reliance on medical records to obtain data for evaluative purposes has proven inadequate, and many people have proposed new, independent record systems for data collection or have suggested improvements in current medical record systems.[8]

There have been several reported efforts in social work to develop information systems which attempt to record and retrieve data which are specific, verifiable, and time-limited statements of interventive activities and goals. Vanderwall[9] and Jack[10] attempted to develop recording systems which could assess social work functions by examining problems with which social workers dealt, the interventions utilized, and outcome of the care provided. The recording systems in these projects enabled data to be collected in an orderly fashion. In and of themselves, the forms could not evaluate process or outcome; they were perceived as mechanisms through which social work data could be documented and retrieved so that evaluation or review could be accomplished. Other, more recent attempts at improving social work information systems may be found in a wide range of social work departments in health care settings.[11] It is interesting to observe that there are more common determinants among them than differences.[12] Each approach focuses on the means of establishing systematic and consistent data retrieval systems which can be integrated into the medical record.

The medical record system and its improvement, long a focus of accrediting bodies, is regarded as an essential foundation for successful professional review systems. With federal, state, and local agencies requiring the monitoring of services and demanding valid auditing systems, the availability of consistent, clear, reliable, and valid data is absolutely essential. Without the means of uniform data retrieval based on predetermined criteria, normative patterns which exist in current service delivery cannot be ascertained. And without such norms the development of standards will continue to depend on highly subjective determinations of acceptable practice, frequently based on traditional values which often do not take into consideration variations between regions or among different types of departments.

Norms, Standards, and Criteria

Any projected review mechanism requires norms, criteria, and standards on which to base review decisions. The federal regulations annotate the need to develop these, stating: "norms, criteria and standards should be developed for each major diagnosis, health problem or procedure which will come under review."[13] The regulations do not limit review to diagnosis solely, but perceive the broader perspective in "problem" or "procedure." To review care, the criteria or the elements in that care need to be established—value judgments explicitly stated and arrived at by professionals to determine that similar situations can be recognized and judged similarly. The criteria can be: outcome (the result at some projected time), process (the "services or behaviors" of the provider), or structure (the health care resources). "Standards are professionally developed expressions of the range of acceptable variations from a norm or a criteria,"[14] the determinants from which the criteria are permitted to deviate. Valid assessment of care depends on the availability of professionally accepted standards of care; the professional providers must agree as to what constitutes good care. Established standards of practice would make possible judgments on whether or not a particular worker or department has fulfilled a commitment to patient care. An evaluative review examines how appropriately and how adequately standards are met; the results of the comparison are used to identify the quality and the problems, so that solutions may be projected.

How are standards arrived at? There have been three generally accepted approaches. One utilizes survey studies which gather large quantities of normative data describing practice and the criteria set for that practice; from these norms, statistical ranges can be determined which then become the accepted standard. A second method is to use expert judges to review written case material or to observe practice; majority judgments may then be utilized or consensus reached among judges as to what are acceptable standards of practice. The third is to select peers from the profession and to seek their agreement as to "good" care in given situations. In all circumstances, the professionals themselves are expected to set standards.

At this time a few survey efforts to uncover normative social work interventive patterns are reported. The University of Virginia, through its regional data retrieval system, can collect large quantities of normative information about delivery of service,[15] but the data collected primarily concerns time factors and includes little information on types of problems dealt with by social workers. Kirstein's work[16] represents another type of effort to analyze norms through a survey of social work intervention. Kirstein assumes that social work delivery patterns will differ by diagnoses; therefore, in order to determine norms, he examines a large number of cases in particular disease groups.

Another attempt using a regional survey approach is the recently completed New England PSRO Survey of Social Work Services to Adult Inpatients.[17] This survey assumes that audit should concern itself with the question of social work's specific contribution to patient-family care that differentiates its service contributions from those of other professions. In order to answer this question, the goals of intervention, the social problems which justify entry into the case, must be explicit. For this reason the survey utilizes a revised version of the Berkman and Rehr social problem classification system.[18]

A prior chapter dealing with a peer review system implemented in The Mount Sinai Department of Social Work Services describes the use of judges to assess practice. Through peer review, good practice, based on judged criteria and standards, can be identified, and, when peer review is refined, it may be possible to draw on that data, as cumulative profiles of social work interventions, thus providing another approach to audit.

Structural Audits

A review of a system's structural components examines the operational framework in which service is delivered. Structural approaches generally focus upon the setting in which care is given and the extent to which these structures have the capacity to provide quality care. The approach has been used frequently because obtaining the data has been relatively easy and inexpensive. In earlier chapters, both Rosenberg and Rehr have identified a number of structural components which can be reviewed, including availability and accessibility of services, staffing patterns, adequacy of recording, and the relevancy of each to measurement of outcome.

The advantage of the structural review lies in its recognition that care is given within the constraints of an organization. However, the questionable basic assumption of such an approach is that good structure is related to good care; in reality, evaluation of structure is probably the most indirect measure of quality of care. The missing link in structural reviews is the necessity first to determine if there is a relationship between structural characteristics and good care. Many professionals assume that professionally based structural standards lead to optimum practice conditions which, in themselves, contribute to good care, but it has been difficult to test, for example, whether the relationship between the provision of privacy in interviewing (a structural factor) and quality of care can be ascertained. In structural reviews comparisons are made, when possible, to structural standards which have a proven effect on the quality of service delivered. An example of a structural review approach, the Service Evaluation and Information System (Sevins), has as its major concern cost effectiveness and provides information for administrative decision making, focusing on client management, use of worker time, and agency finances.[19] Spano and Lund,[20] using Management by Objectives (MBO) in their structural approach, stipulate that a department must state its philosophy, define its functions, and set up a procedure to establish yearly objectives and goals. Professional activities are placed in specific categories based upon standards consistent with the agency's objectives.

Structural audits have value even though they may not be predictive of the quality of outcome. They do permit an evaluation of the environment and resources of the system of care. A professionally determined optimum structure for practice is certainly a sought-after objective of every practitioner.

Process Audits

In the audit of processes of care, the procedures or performance of staff are evaluated. A process assessment permits review of the care which is or has actually been provided and the means by which the patient is or was treated. Process is regarded as a sequence of acts or interventions in the delivery of care, diagnostic and therapeutic interventions on behalf of a patient. In social work, process has been measured in terms of time allocations, such as units of interview time, in terms of modalities such as casework, group therapy, or family therapy, or in terms of defined interventions such as face-to-face contacts, telephone, and so on. If at the present time social work were to rely solely on process or performance accountability, the profession would have little to offer apart from the structural units of measures. Social work has yet to define uniform and acceptable criteria for and standards of process, although efforts to do so are under way.[20] An example of explicit criteria for social work practice is proposed by Meites,[21] who delineates five interventive modalities for use in patient care, the choice of which is determined by the psycho-social diagnosis. However, where standards and criteria are expressed, they are generally based upon theoretical and traditional values which may or may not be related to normative practice.

Some professionals believe that process and outcome are highly related. However, this has been demonstrated only in the clear-cut cause-and-effect situations when the intervention given, such as immunization (process) administered for prevention of polio, leads to the desired effect, less polio (outcome) in a population. When performance or process is the critical means of assessment, the findings in relation to outcome have generally been inconclusive. Intervening factors such as sociodemographic and psychological variables may be equally (or more) meaningful with respect to sustaining of care and of outcome. Most evaluations of quality of care in regard to social work practices in health care settings have dealt with professional performance; few evaluative studies have used end results or outcome of care. Performance assessment, the traditional method used in supervision, clearly has not concentrated on outcome at all. The linkage between performance and outcome is obviously needed.

Outcome Audit

The third approach to audit involves outcome review: examination of the outcome of services delivered, assessing the status of individuals along some clearly defined lines after social work intervention. Outcome studies are often considered the elite of review systems, since they are supposed to answer directly the question of the effectiveness of the service given. Outcome reviews, however, are frequently expensive and methodologically complex.

At present, there are no uniform or generalizable approaches for measuring the outcome of social work interventions. There are a wide range of experimental approaches, each with its error potential, advantages, and disadvantages.[22]

Three major problems hinder devising a method for assessment of outcome. The first problem is the difficulty of defining "outcome"—a term defined quite differently by different researchers in different settings. Many forces influence the definition: social and cultural values, type of setting and types of patients, and various other administrative concerns. The reviewers must decide where to focus the outcome assessment: in the individual or client system, in the instrumentalities for services, or in environmental-social adjustment terms.[23] The second obstacle to outcome studies lies in the failure to develop satisfactory tools of measurement. Closely related is the added methodological problem of determining whether extraneous factors, such as environmental or psychological variables, did not have as much or more effect on outcome as the interventive practice itself.

Kiresuk summarizes the complex demands on outcome measures:

The measure would have to satisfy the usual criteria standards of psychological measurement, be relevant and meaningful to therapists, be useful in research, meet administrative needs, be capable of numerical relationship to process measures and resources allocation, be comprehensible to patients and consumer representatives, and be related to rationale management and scientific inquiry while retaining the sweet mystery of life. There is no such measure, of course.[24]

Because of such problems many reviewers have relied on a process or structural review approach as the means of evaluation.[25] Given these problems, however, different competent approaches to reviewing outcome have been reported: each possesses its merits and deficits. Judges, one widely used method of assessment, can employ clients themselves through self ratings,[26] or can rely on staff judgments,[27] or the judgment of appropriate "other" persons as in the Sickness Impact Profile Approach.[28] In the consumer evaluation method, the client serves as a valid source of review for such factors as availability of services, continuity, and comprehensiveness of care; in fact, the consumer does assess services received and decides whether to return and whether to recommend the service to others. Studies by Kisch and Reeder[29] and Reinherz[30] strongly indicate a high degree of consumer accuracy in service evaluation. Comparing consumer assessment of outcome with worker assessment would provide a measure of validity to the outcome judgment.

Another approach to outcome which has received serious consideration is reported by Kiresuk as a standardized approach called Goal Attainment Scaling (GAS).[31] This innovative approach to assessment of services is now being used by a number of professional groups and different agencies, but with considerable local adaptation.[32] GAS can be described briefly as a technique wherein the selection of goals is made by the worker either alone or in conjunction with the client at the beginning of treatment. Next, the worker, or worker and client, predicts the most likely outcome for each goal and develops a range of possible outcomes around that goal. This then permits an objective audit of goal achievement at the conclusion of treatment. GAS is not a complete audit mechanism but an extremely important and useful instrument in dealing with performance, predictability, and outcome.

The Mount Sinai Social Health Care
Evaluation

It is the premise of The Mount Sinai Hospital Department of Social Work Services that, in order to conduct a meaningful audit of its services, descriptive data must be collected on: patients served; interventive activities, including interviews and modalities utilized; social problems dealt with; and outcome of intervention. The Department has designed a data retrieval system which brings a continuous flow of this type of case information. Through the continuous documentation and retrieval of large quantities of case data on social worker interventive patterns, the Department will eventually determine its own normative patterns of intervention in relation to particular types of case situations— one means by which standards and criteria will be promulgated within this hospital's structure and service patterns. The peer review system previously described will reinforce clinical normative patterns, through the gathering and assessment of cumulative practice profiles.

The Department has just completed its first Social Health Care Evaluation,[33] reviewing the "contracts" (agreements on problems to be dealt with) between social workers and their clients, and the outcomes social workers ascribe to their work. This study established an audit methodology to meet the mandated requirements for examining the delivery of social work services in the institution. The first set of review questions asked focused on both process and outcome of intervention.

1. What social problem "contracts" for social work were made between worker and client?
2. What interventive activities were utilized?
3. Do normative ranges of interventive patterns differ, depending on number of contracts or by disease entity?
4. Do social worker "outcomes" vary according to types of psycho-social problems?

The audit involved four phases of data collection. Phase I documented the types of case situations opened by master's degreed social workers on the medical and surgical inpatient services during a one-month study period. The social worker was asked to specify, utilizing the Berkman-Rehr classification of social problems,[34] the initial problems-contracts for service agreed to between worker and client. This original social problem-contract classification has been revised on the basis of staff suggestions and includes the entire range of problems for all types of individuals and services. (See Exhibit 8.)

Phase II collected data at case closing on the social workers' perceptions of outcome of intervention in relation to the specific "contracts" identified in Phase I. The workers also added and judged outcome on any contracts made after those recorded in Phase I. Workers could select from four discrete categories of outcome that which described their assessment of the end result of their intervention. These categories were: "resolved" or "improved" (the problem was solved or alleviated); "unchanged"; "deferred" (both the social worker and client, or either, decided not to pursue the contract); and "no longer applicable" (the contract no longer applied, such as in the case of a patient who needed a nursing home but died during hospitalization, or a change in the focus of intervention by the worker or client). This outcome classification system has been revised based on changes suggested by staff (Exhibit 8).

Phase III of data collection utilized Mount Sinai's computerized social work statistical system through which sociodemographic information is available on each patient known to the Department, as well as social worker intervention data such as: number of client "in-person" interviews and number of supportive ("other" interviews and telephone contacts) services. (See Exhibits 3, 4, and 5.)

Obtaining data by case on patient profiles, worker activity patterns, and contracted social needs and outcome of intervention permitted the type of statistical analysis which was essential for the audit. In addition to its quantity assessment capability, systemizing data collection is considered a necessary step in the development of standards for social work intervention. Specific delineation of social problems in the context of illness and the outcome of intervention directly related to those problems are also essential components of this system. The audit approach is predicated on all these factors and on a need to assess end results or outcome of care in direct relation to the goal of service delivery.

Phase IV involved a validity study of the social workers' perception of contract and assessment of outcome. Clients served as sources for validating the social workers' judgments and were interviewed by telephone within three weeks of case closing. The clients' understanding of the problems dealt with, as agreed to between the workers and themselves, and their assessment of the outcome of social work services, as specifically related to the identified problems, were explored in brief telephone interviews conducted by a trained interviewer. (See Exhibit 9.)

The findings of this first Social Health Care Evaluation have dramatic implications. The study assumed that the client can be the primary source validating the social worker's perceptions of social problems dealt with and assessments of outcome of intervention. Comparing client assessment of outcome with worker assessment provides a meaningful measure of validity. The findings of the client follow-up permit no question that social worker judgment of case contract and outcome of intervention are valid. Worker training in contractual intervention has resulted in substantial agreement between clients and social workers on the problems with and the outcomes of intervention (91 percent and 86 percent agreement, respectively). The authors believe that a combination of worker ratings of outcome combined with random client validation is a viable means of professional review. The Department plans to initiate such a system as an integral part of its continuous process of data retrieval and a comparatively inexpensive means of describing the developing role of the social work program in meeting clients' needs.

One system of evaluation, the authors believe, should be based on social problem to outcome measures. That it is possible to conduct a viable audit of social work service delivery has been demonstrated.[35] When problems or goals are stated in clearly defined, limited terms, they can more readily be judged as to goal attainment. Some critics of this approach believe that specific classification of social problems and outcome tends to partialize or fragment the individual and suggest that the practitioner suffers in moving to a narrow, incomplete view of clients rather than a holistic approach. Experience shows that this approach does permit some goal attainment judgment on one or more specific objectives or contracts. When there is more than one "contract," then the assessment is specified in sequential tasks and their resolutions. This sequential contracting, it has been suggested, provides "rolling objectives" agreed on between worker and client for problem resolution within the time span negotiated.

The first Mount Sinai audit of social work services generated important, previously unavailable practice findings. Table 1

TABLE 1

Contractual "Outcomes" by Number of Problem-Contracts in Case Service Patterns, and Patient's Length of Stay

Number of Problem-Contracts	Contractual Outcome				Service Patterns		
	Resolved/ Improved (%)	Unchanged (%)	Deferred (%)	No Longer Applicable (%)	Ave. No. Interv. Per Case	Ave. No. Supp. Per Case	Ave. LOS Per Case
1	79	8	4	9	4.5	10.16	29.18
2	63	17	4	16	6.4	11.14	32.61
3 or more	56	24	3	17	10.4	23.56	38.62
Total Problem-Contracts (N = 350)	63	19	3	15	8.5	13.01	33.40
Initials (N = 112 Cases)	64	15	3	18	5.78*	10.25**	30.29***
Sequentials (N = 60 Cases)	60	27	3	10	11.01*	21.43**	38.01***

* = (t = −3.59, df = 170, $P \leq$ .001)
** = (t = −4.83, df = 170, $P \leq$ .001)
*** = (t = −1.95, df = 156, $P \leq$ .05) (df less because we could not locate length of stay records for 14 patients)

Reprinted with permission of *Social Work in Health Care*, March 1978, Vol. 3, No. 3, p. 282.

offers only one example of the types of information accumulated during the efforts to learn normative patterns of intervention on which to base standards and criteria. The data displayed in this table highlight the audit question of whether interventive patterns differ with the number of contracts and length of hospitalization. A relationship exists between length of stay, number of contracts, and intervention patterns: the average number of interviews with patients and family members and the average number of supportive services increase with an increasing number of problem contracts and with an increase in the average length of stay.

The advantages of problem classification linked to outcome classification as a method of review are that of clarity and relevance for other professionals and for consumers who tend to assess in terms of specific problem categories and specific outcomes. This first evaluation has been presented at the Hospital's Medical Audit Committee, in conformity with and fulfilling medical care evaluation requirements. One of the serendipitous results was the unqualified positive response of physicians to social problem classification as a classification of social work interventive areas; they viewed it as a significant interpretation of social services. A second result was the request to include the projected utilization of the SHCE as a methodology in an interdisciplinary audit dealing with the disease-specific of diabetes. This form of social work audit—statement of the mutually agreed-upon problem and judgment of outcome—lends itself to easy collection of data and does not require formal research or professional review. When it has been completed, the Berkman-Rehr problem outcome classification can be reviewed by medical record librarians, who are now undertaking medical care evaluation, while final interpretation and significance of the findings would be professionally reviewed. Final assessment with its implications for change is shared with the social work staff.

Social health care evaluations possess relevance and relationship to medical care evaluations conducted in a medical institution. The authors continue to base this audit on a frame of reference derived from social work and will include a problem (contract) outcome instrument which can be integrated into any nursing or medical audit. The Berkman and Rehr social problem classification system has been revised to apply to all patients, regardless of age, physical disease, disorder or disability, who enter the social work service system of the Mount Sinai Medical Center. The instrument used in the first Mount Sinai Hospital Social Health Care Evaluation represents an orderly methodological system for data collection, clearly delineating a professional assessment of social work delivery of services specific to the social health problems of patients and families served by the Hospital.

References

1. *Evaluation,* published by Program Evaluation Resource Center, of the Minneapolis Medical Research Foundation, Inc., in collaboration with the National Institute of Mental Health, Mental Health Service Development Branch (501 South Park Avenue, Minneapolis, Minnesota 55415).

2. PSRO Program Manual, Chapter VII, Section 709, Chapter VII, pp. 16–20.

3. *Ibid.,* Section 730, Chapter VII, pp. 31–33.

4. *Ibid.,* Section 730.52–730.54.

5. Abraham Lurie, "Social Service Conducts Two Quality Assurance Programs," *Hospitals,* Feb. 1, 1978, Vol. 52, p. 67.

6. Jerrold Kirstein, *Research Studies I Through V and Narrative Article.* Washington, D.C., National Association of Social Workers, October 1975.

7. Helen Rehr, "Professional Standards Review and Utilization Review: The Challenge to Social Work," *Development of Professional Standards Review,* Chicago, Illinois, American Hospital Association, 1977, pp. 23–36; Barbara Berkman, and Helen Rehr, "Social Work Undertakes Its Own Audit," *Social Work in Health Care,* Vol. 3 (3) March 1978, pp. 273–286.

8. David Wirtschafter, and Emmanuel Mesel, "A Strategy for Redesigning the Medical Record for Quality Assurance," *Medical Care,* January 1976, Vol. 14, pp. 68–76; Martin Nacman, *Notes on the Implementation of Quality Control,* Rochester, New York, Strong Memorial Hospital, 1976.

9. William Vanderwall, "Accountability of Social Services in a Health Program: A Working Model," *Accountability: A Critical Issue in Social Services,* edited by William T. Hall and Gerald C. St. Denis, University of Pittsburgh, Pennsylvania, Graduate School of Public Health, 1972, pp. 46–60.

10. Bonnie Jack, "Social Work Accountability in a Children and Youth Project," *Accountability: A Critical Issue in Social Services,* edited by William T. Hall and Gerald C. St. Denis, University of Pittsburgh, Pennsylvania, Graduate School of Public Health, 1972, pp. 35–45.

11. Claudia J. Coulton, *Social Work Quality Assurance Program: A Comparative Analysis,* prepared for Committee on Health Quality Standards, Washington, D.C., National Association of Social Workers, 1978.

12. See Mabel Meites, "One Adaptation of Social Work to a Peer Review System," *PSRO Newsletter,* NASW, No. 4:14, May 1976; K. Ferguson, et al., "Initiation Of A Quality Assurance Program For Social Work Practice In A Teaching Hospital," *Social Work in Health Care,* Vol. 2(2), Winter 1976–77, pp. 205–217; D.B. Black, et al., "Model For Clinical Social Work Practice In A Health Care Facility," *Social Work in Health Care,* Vol. 3(2), Winter 1977, pp. 143–148; R.M. Spano, et al., "An Operational Model To Achieve Accountability For Social Work In Health Care," *Social Work in Health Care,* Vol. 3(2) Winter 1977, pp. 123–140; Patricia Volland, "Social Work Information and Accountability In A Hospital Setting," *Social Work in Health Care,* Vol. 1(3), Spring 1977, pp. 277–285; B. Berkman, "Are Social Work Audit Systems Feasible?" *Development of Professional Standards Review,* Chicago, Ill., American Hospital Association, 1977, pp. 37–43.

13. *PSRO Program Manual,* Section 709.13, Chapter VII, p. 17.

14. Project to Develop Model Criteria and Standards for Care of End-Stage Renal Disease Patients, California Committee on Regional Medical Programs, Inc., Box 6059, Oakland, Calif. 94614, pp. 9–52.

15. "University of Virginia Uses Computer to Set Up Time, Work Norms," *NASW News,* Washington, D.C., June 1975, p. 9.

16. Kirstein, *op. cit.,* pp. 1–19.

17. Berkman, *op. cit.,* 1977, pp. 37–43.

18. Barbara Berkman, and Helen Rehr, "Social Needs of the Hospitalized Elderly: A Classification," *Social Work,* Vol. 17, No. 4, July 1972, pp. 80–88.

19. Edith Fein, "A Data System for an Agency," *Social Work,* January 1975, Vol. 20, No. 1, pp. 21–24.

20. Robert M. Spano, and Sandra H. Lund, "Management by Objectives in a Hospital Social Service Unit," *Social Work in Health Care,* Spring, 1976, Vol. 1, No. 3, pp. 267–276.

21. Mabel Meites, "One Adaptation of Social Work to a Peer Review System," *PSRO,* No. 4, 1976, NASW, Washington, D.C.

22. Claudia J. Coulton, and Phyllis L. Solomon, "Measuring Outcome of Intervention," *Social Work Research and Abstracts,* Vol. 13, No. 4, Winter 1977, pp. 3–9.

23. Avedis Donabedian, "Measuring and Evaluating Hospital and Medical Care," *Bulletin of the New York Academy of Medicine,* Vol. 52(1), Jan. 1976, p. 51.

24. Thomas Kiresuk, "Goal Attainment Scaling at a County Mental Health Service," *Evaluation,* January 1973, pp. 12–18.

25. Alex Richman, and Henry Pinsker, "Medical Audit by Clinical Rounds," *American Journal of Psychiatry,* December 1974, Vol. 131, No. 12, pp. 1370–1374.

26. Evelyn Ogren, "Sample Bias in Patient Evaluation of Hospital Social Ser-

vices," *Social Work in Health Care,* Fall 1975, Vol. 1, No. 1, pp. 55–65; Deborah Blumberg, et al., "Clients' Evaluation of Medical Social Services," *Social Work,* January 1975, Vol. 20, No. 1, pp. 45–47.

27. Barbara Starfield, "Measurement of Outcome: A Proposed Scheme," *The Milbank Memorial Fund Quarterly/Health and Society,* Winter 1974, Vol. 52, No. 1, pp. 39–50.

28. Betty Gilson, et al., "The Sickness Impact Profile—Development of an Outcome Measure of Health Care," *American Journal of Public Health,* December 1975, Vol. 65, No. 12, pp. 1304–1310.

29. Arnold Kisch, and Leo Reeder, "Client Evaluation of Physician Performance," *Journal of Health and Social Behavior,* Vol. 10, No. 1, March 1965, pp. 51–58.

30. Helen Reinherz, "Shared Perspectives—A Community Counseling Center for Adolescents," *Adolescence,* Vol. XI, No. 42, Summer 1976, pp. 167–179.

31. Kiresuk, *op. cit.*

32. Edward M. Glaser, and Thomas E. Backer, "Innovation Redefined: Desirability and Local Adaptation," *Evaluation,* Vol. 4, 1977, p. 133.

33. Barbara Berkman, and Helen Rehr, "Social Work Undertakes its Own Audit," *Social Work in Health Care,* Vol. 3, No. 3, March 1978, pp. 273–286.

34. Berkman and Rehr, *op. cit.,* 1972.

35. Berkman and Rehr, *op. cit.,* 1978.

8

Continuing Education and the Self-Directed Worker

GARY ROSENBERG

Continuing education, peer review, and the self-directed worker concept can be linked in a triadic relationship. The PSRO manual links peer review and continuing education and Epstein has linked continuing education and the self-directed worker:

Increased opportunities for autonomous practice in the future will depend on two changes: (1) decentralization of bureaucratic authority and responsibility and (2) abandonment of the obligatory teaching-learning posture as the major means of controlling professional behavior. Decentralization is a matter of organizational policy and design. . . . Not only is ongoing professional education the individual practitioner's responsibility, it is the only way that such education can occur under any conditions. However, for practitioners to avail themselves of continuing education, the opportunities must be available, accessible, attractive, and divorced from mandatory tutorial education.[1]

This chapter describes the creation of a continuing education program, linked to peer review, with the goal of contributing to development of social workers' self-directedness.

There is a strong national interest in continuing education for the professions. For a long time this need for continuing education of the agency staffs and departments of social work has been answered through orientation programs, in-service education, consultations, and links with schools of social work for post-graduate training and education.[2]

The literature elucidates the purposes and needs which these programs are designed to fulfill:

1. There is an explosion of new knowledge and consequently the need to apply such knowledge in practice.[3]
2. The degree programs (MSW, BSW) now educate practitioners to recognize that degree attainment is not the end of education and learning.[4]

3. Continuing currency and relevancy are fundamental to socialization into professional status.[5]

4. To offer innovative and relevant services, organizations need staff who have new knowledge and who can deepen existing knowledge.

5. Salary raises and promotions are part of institutional arrangements in the outcomes of continuing education.[6]

6. Continuing education stimulates innovation in practice and research.

7. In some states licensing and certification of the professions require continuing education; all states are expected to adopt it eventually, with the endorsement of the professional societies.

8. Primary vendor payments from insurance companies require evidence of adherence to professional standards review, of which one requisite is continuing education.

9. PSRO legislation requires continuing education based on feedback from the results of peer review or audit of services developed under professional review.

The remainder of this chapter discusses the underlying principles used in formulating the continuing education program of one Department of Social Work Services, the program's content, the efforts employed to plan curriculum and to develop a qualified faculty, and the strategies of evaluation.

Principles for the Development of a
Continuing Education Program

Development of the continuing education program for social work emphasizing self-directedness as a joint staff-administration project began to flourish in 1976, the result of many years of administrative commitment to staff development through provision of educational opportunity as an institutional responsibility. This commitment was rooted in the belief that the social worker, as do other professionals, must possess current, relevant knowledge in order to practice effectively.

By requesting volunteers from among staff already interested in such a program, a planning group was formed. These principles guided the efforts of the planning group:

1. Seminars linked to peer review and audit were necessary to educate staff for excellence in practice, and participation in and contribution to their own educational development.

2. What needed to be learned would be based on multiple inputs to the system, including social worker judgment, peer review and audit, staff evaluations, and observations of clinical practice.

3. The educational experiences provided would adhere to principles employed in teaching adults, including a clear understanding of the rights and responsibilities of learner and teacher.[7]

4. A major goal of the continuing education program would be the development of a self-directed worker, responsible for his own practice, and accountable for learning and performance through quantitative and qualitative measures.[8] Peer review, open precepting (teaching), the use of live material—observation, audio, and video tapes —would provide some measure of qualitative accountability.

5. Principles of curriculum planning would be applied to the continuing education program. Curriculum planning was defined as "a matter of curriculum choices and programming in the light of facts, projections and the application of professional values, taking into account the dynamics of institutional infrastructure."[9]

6. A program for faculty development would run concurrently with the seminars, its goal to be teaching how to teach.[10] Only those who demonstrated an ability to teach, as measured by agreed-upon outcomes, would be retained as faculty. As Frey stated, "the good teacher, whether a novice or experienced, must have a desire to teach and a capacity to communicate directly in an educational transaction with active learners. He or she must have the ability to conceptualize knowledge and engage in an intellectually and emotionally challenging process."[11]

Curriculum Planning

Two approaches were used in the curriculum. A two-semester seminar program, based on the principles stated, was planned by a combined staff and faculty group in seven weekly meetings. The faculty was chosen, after consultation with staff and administration, by the author who was administratively responsible for the continuing education program.

The first semester was planned as a set of general seminars using, as the conceptual base for teaching, the Department's peer review model for evaluation. The second set of seminars was designed to follow the same conceptual framework but to teach specific techniques or problem-focused practice.

The Seminar Program

The author believes that continuing education in health care must build upon the knowledge, skills, and values which social workers bring to the health care setting, and should be carried out in a time-phased program.

The following skill areas were designated as the focus for teaching content in the seminar program:

1. *Entry and Assessment Skills*—These include developing a framework for making assessments and identifying key factors in the presenting situations of the patient/family; sifting through information obtained to focus on problem formulation and resolution; selecting appropriate problems on which to work; assessing problems in relation to level of functioning, patterns of relationships, and strengths, as well as problem areas, in the patient and his social system; assessing with whom to work and what would constitute a measure of success. Assessments must, the author believes, be framed with conceptual clarity and precision and must lead to problem formulation, with the expected resolution stated.

2. *Collaborative Practice*—This area involved the recognition that most social workers in health care, while functioning as autonomous professionals, independent from physicians, must develop collaborative skills in order to

make a full assessment, as well as to contribute essential information to the health care team.

3. *Contracting with the Client*—This skill is based on the worker's ability to formulate problems and to develop initial and sequential contracts with the patient about the problems identified. Time and participation of the patient in contracting, constitute major factors in determining success.

4. *Intervention Skills*—These include selection of appropriate interventions to be used for the client, at the proper moment and for a suitable period of time. Interventions flow clearly from assessments, i.e., clearly formulated problems, collaborative practices, contracting, and established goals. Techniques are devised to conceptualize the problem appropriately in order to make it resolvable. Workers should be trained to direct interventions toward the social context of the patient, his family, or other social systems. It is the social worker's task to formulate a presenting problem clearly and to design an intervention, in the patient's social situation, to change it accordingly.[12]

5. *Evaluation of Outcomes*—This area includes teaching workers to evaluate the outcome of treatment in simple terms: the types of intervention used; their appropriateness; the worker's satisfaction with outcome; the client's satisfaction with outcome; the possibility of handling the problem differently, and how that might be done.

6. *Recording Skills*—This area emphasizes how to record in the patient's chart, clearly and concisely, the following information: entry and assessment; collaborative efforts; problems formulated, contracts, interventions, and the evaluation of treatment processes; outcomes. Good recording requires conceptual clarity in stating these phases of treatment.

During the first semester, five seminars were offered, each on a different day. Since the seminars were designed to be similar in content, workers selected the most convenient time; faculty had not yet been announced and was not a factor in this first selection. For the second set of seminars, this policy was changed, since staff wished to be able to select a seminar topic of interest with a specific faculty member.

The first small group seminars focused on skill development, using material which included live interviews, audio tapes, video tapes, and patient and family interviews behind one-way mirrors. Appropriate release forms were obtained from the clients. These measures were utilized to help the social worker to improve his skills through direct observation by an expert in teaching. In addition to assisting the workers to understand their feelings or the relationship factors in the case, the teacher can offer active ways to resolve problems presented by the patient/family. After each particular interview, a chart note was written and presented at the beginning of the next seminar meeting. Teaching then focused on aiding the social worker to conceptualize practice and to write a concise, accurate chart note which communicated to the health care team the essence of what had transpired.

A second set of seminars focused either on the application of these skills to the specialized techniques of family therapy, group treatment, crisis and short-term therapy, and marital counseling, or on work with such specific problems as those of the aging, chronic illness, or acute life-threatening conditions.

Open Precepting

Concurrent with the seminar program, a change was made in the traditional supervisory functions of the Department. Under the previous system, administrative and teaching functions resided in the same person. This system was considered antiquated in that no one person could teach everything well and that it fostered a mutual dependency between supervisor and worker, since each needed each other for adequate role performance in the role set.[13]

This system also impeded development of the self-directed professional, defined as one who is responsible for his or her own practice.[14] Responsibility for one's own practice means the capacity to use knowledge as a practice guide, to accept the responsibility for actions and outcomes, with a commitment to self-evaluation and self-improvement. The self-directed worker is a departmental goal, which can be achieved.[15]

The new system, called open precepting, expanded learning opportunities by making expert teaching available on a tutorial or small-group basis. Each former supervisor, now termed "preceptor," was given the task of developing expertise in teaching specific content, such areas as: the impact of physical illness on the patient and family, family treatment, child treatment, collaborative practice, short-term treatment, entry and assessment skills, treatment of sexual dysfunctions, ego psychology, social rehabilitation techniques, advocacy, and so on. Now the social worker had opportunities to learn from a variety of people; the worker was expected to take the initiative in identifying his own learning needs and to contract with the preceptors accordingly. Teaching and administrative staff could assist the worker to identify these needs and the faculty appropriate to the learning effort.

Once learning need and preceptor were identified, a contract was written specifying the learning and teaching on which both parties agreed to work (see Exhibit 17); the contract included a general statement of the area to be learned, followed by specific learning goals. At the end of the contract period, the preceptor and the worker assessed the amount of learning that had taken place, any further learning that was needed, and whether the worker would continue, or move on to another area with another preceptor. Whether time limits must be set for open precepting remains an undecided issue.

Faculty Development Seminars

Weekly meetings were held to assist faculty, mainly preceptors, to learn classroom teaching techniques and to develop a philosophy of continuing education. The philosophy is embodied in the work of Frey:

The worker as an adult is motivated to learn, can participate in his own learning, and has responsibility to help determine what he needs and wants to learn. These assumptions mandate educational structures that permit openness, collaborative learning, reciprocity, and, in essence, an interdependence between the educator and the participants. The role of the educator of adults is multiple: resource, enabler, expert, structurer, guide, teacher, learner. The assumptions reflect the values of creativity, intellectual curiosity, respect for the individual, self-determination, and responsibility for assisting in the learning of others. If agencies want to offer educational programs that will reach adult learners, they must develop teachers who can use modern methods of education and who know how to set achievable education objectives and how to organize course content relevant to the needs of the learners.[16]

A bibliography on teaching was developed and distributed and discussions held on educating workers rather than supervising cases. The discussions centered on teaching workers how to identify problems, locate obstacles to problem solving, assist patients in problem solving, and evaluate the results of their work.

Video tapes of teaching were presented and discussed and bibliographies developed for the teaching modules. Other skills and techniques taught included use of audio and video tapes and of professional literature in teaching, teaching from chart notes, knowledge of group process, and the developmental phases of groups. Both seminar teaching and open precepting were covered.

As the seminars continued, teaching staff taped their sessions, visited each other's groups, and invited the faculty seminar leader (the author) to observe their teaching. These experiences nourished the ongoing faculty development seminar, where they could be translated into teaching skills for the faculty, i.e., how the faculty was taught and learned served as a model for teaching the seminar groups.

Strategies of Evaluation

Evaluating a continuing education program raises many problems. As Whitaker says:

> Practically no evaluation has been made of the effectiveness of the programs in terms of changed behavior or of improvements in quality of the health care. Evaluation tools to measure the results of the instruction, looking for evidence of application of the new knowledge to one's practice, need to be developed. At present, attendance is the criterion used as the major measuring rod to judge the program's worth.[17]

While the Department wished to follow classic scientific methodology in testing its efforts in continuing education, this was regarded as feasible in a later phase of the experience.

In considering the choices for evaluation strategies, two sources seemed most promising. The first was an evaluation by the social workers participating in the program. The second was to measure by peer review the improvement in practice of the seminar members and compare them to a group not exposed to departmental continuing education. The latter approach presented design problems and is yet to be implemented.

As a first step in attempting to measure the outcome of this program, a form to measure the social worker's satisfaction with this type of continuing education was created (see Exhibit 18). The components of the form include: the goals of the participants, the participants' gains from the seminar, assessment of the group process, assessment of the faculty, and assessment of the content taught and learned. The forms were filled out without the names of the participants; only the seminar number and faculty member identified the group. Tables 2 and 3 describe the participants' overall reactions to learning as a whole and by each seminar group. The results have been encouraging. Sixty-six percent of the staff rated the experience as good or outstanding in the areas of skill enhancement and acquisition of new ideas.

Table 4 shows that seventy-five percent of the participants believed their own group to be supportive in encouraging participation.

Table 5 is a global rating scale of instructors. With the exception of seminar groups A and E, the majority of the participants believed the instructors to be outstanding; all the participants rated the instructor in seminar group E as good.

In Table 6 the participants rated achievement of their learning goals. Sixty-six percent of the respondents rated it as good or outstanding; only 7 percent rated it inadequate, and all of those were in seminars A and E. The evaluations of the second set of seminars showed an increase in satisfaction in all areas, but the increase was not at a statistically significant level.

The overall impressions were that the faculty effort has been successful in engaging the participants in setting learning goals, participating in creating a group atmosphere conducive to learning, and acquiring new skills for practice. A word of caution must be given regarding the meaning of these results: they have not demonstrated a transfer to practice; there is no objective evidence that patient care has been improved. A rating change by one person could significantly change the seminar group rating because of the small number of participants. While the overall ratings may be more valid as a description of the total staff experience, the data on each group served as evaluative information for the seminar leaders in regard to their teaching skills.

TABLE 2

Assessment of "Enhancement of Skills"

ASSESSMENT	GROUP					
	A (N = 10) %	B (N = 8) %	C (N = 6) %	D (N = 10) %	E (N = 7) %	Total (N = 41) %
Inadequate	50	—	—	—	—	12
Adequate	50	—	—	10	43	22
Good	—	62	100	10	57	39
Outstanding	—	38	—	80	—	27
TOTAL	100	100	100	100	100	100

TABLE 3

Assessment of "Introduction of New Ideas"

ASSESSMENT	GROUP					
	A (N = 10) %	B (N = 8) %	C (N = 6) %	D (N = 10) %	E (N = 7) %	Total (N = 41) %
Inadequate	80	—	—	—	14	22
Adequate	—	13	17	—	43	12
Good	20	62	66	40	43	44
Outstanding	—	25	17	60	—	22
TOTAL	100	100	100	100	100	100

TABLE 4

Assessment of "Groups Support for Encouraging Participation"

ASSESSMENT	A (N = 10) %	B (N = 8) %	C (N = 6) %	D (N = 10) %	E (N = 7) %	Total (N = 41) %
Inadequate	10	—	—	—	14	4
Adequate	40	38	—	—	—	19
Good	40	50	33	50	43	43
Outstanding	—	12	67	50	43	32
NA	10	—	—	—	—	2
TOTAL	100	100	100	100	100	100

TABLE 5

Assessment of "Overall Rating of Instructor" by Group Members

ASSESSMENT	GROUP					
	A (N = 10) %	B (N = 8) %	C (N = 6) %	D (N = 10) %	E (N = 7) %	Total (N = 41) %
Inadequate	80	—	—	—	—	20
Adequate	10	—	—	—	—	2
Good	10	25	33	10	100	32
Outstanding	—	75	67	90	—	46
TOTAL	100	100	100	100	100	100

TABLE 6

Assessment of "Groups Accomplishment of Learning Goals" by Group Members

ASSESSMENT	GROUP					
	A (N = 10) %	B (N = 8) %	C (N = 6) %	D (N = 10) %	E (N = 7) %	Total (N = 41) %
Inadequate	10	—	—	—	29	7
Adequate	60	—	16	—	14	20
Good	20	63	50	40	57	44
Outstanding	—	25	16	50	—	20
NA	10	12	16	10	—	9
TOTAL	100	100	98	100	100	100

In order to determine the effect of continuing education on patient care, two sources will be consulted: a client satisfaction study[18] will be reinstituted; the peer review scores over time will be measured to test improvement. The Department hopes to institute both measures in 1978–1979. Until then, it must be cognizant of the phenomena that Kaplan so accurately identifies: "There are many ways we can fool ourselves without objective evaluations. How often do we take credit for solving problems that spontaneously resolve themselves."[19]

The Self-Directed Worker

The continuing education program at The Mount Sinai Hospital has benefitted from the conceptual basis of peer review. Peer review criteria for non-physician health care practitioners are based on an organizational framework created for physician peer review. This development has provided the profession of social work with further opportunity to change some of the concepts of social work in health care delivery, the organizational structure of delivery, and the structure of continuing education for social work practitioners, by strengthening accountability to each other as well as to a hierarchial administrative structure. It has contributed to the continuing education of professional staff through the results of assessment.

This chapter has described the beginning of a continuing education program based in part on a concurrently developing peer review system. By combining a seminar program with an open precepting model, and by creating feedback mechanisms through peer review and audits, the social worker has been furnished with most of the structure needed to become responsible for learning and achieving quality professional practice.

It has been difficult to effect the change from supervisors into teachers through faculty development seminars and equally difficult to convince staff members, accustomed to the former supervisory system, that education for quality professionalism is lodged in a participatory adult education program, in which they share responsibility for curriculum development.

The Department is encouraged by the efforts to date of both teachers and staff to bridge the conceptual and structural gaps in the system, leading to what Epstein has identified as the criteria for the self-directed worker—a shift toward decentralization of authority and an available, attractive educational system. Concepts of peer review, applied to a continuing education program, have given energy, form, and substance to the growth of self-directed workers. The confluence of these three conceptual and structural systems provides new stimulus to work in a health care setting.

References

1. Laura Epstein, "Is Autonomous Practice Possible?" *Social Work*, Vol. 18, No. 2, March 1973, pp. 5–13.

2. Richard J. Estes, "Learning Style Preferences of Community Mental Health Professionals," *Community Mental Health Journal*, Vol. 11, No. 4, 1975, pp. 450–463.

3. Lois G. Swack, "Continuing Education and Changing Needs," *Social Work*, Vol. 20, No. 6, November 1975, pp. 474–480.

4. *Ibid.*

5. Victor Howery, "Continuing Education: Program Development, Administration and Financing," *Education for Social Work*, Winter 1974, pp. 34–41.

6. Melvin N. Brenner, and William H. Koch, "Continuing Education Among Social Workers: Patterns and Profiles," *Approaches to Innovation in Social Work Education*, New York, Council on Social Work Education, 1974, pp. 26–37.

7. Louise L. Cady, "The Philosophy of In-Service and Continuing Education," *Mental Hygiene*, Vol. 52, No. 3, July 1968, pp. 456–461; Merle M. Foeckler, and Gerald Boynton, "Creative Adult Learning-Teaching: Who's the Engineer of this Train?" *Journal of Education for Social Work*, Fall 1976, Vol. 12, No. 3, pp. 37–43.

8. Helen Rehr, "Quality and Quantity Assurance: Issues for Social Services," in *Quality Assurance in Social Services in Health Programs for Mothers and Children*, Pittsburgh, University of Pittsburgh School of Public Health, 1975, pp. 35–47.

9. Beulah Rothman, and Joseph L. Vigilante, "Curriculum Planning in Social Work Education," *Journal of Education for Social Work*, Vol. 10, No. 2, Spring 1974, pp. 76–85.

10. Louise A. Frey, "The Evaluation of Teacher Competence in Continuing Education," *Social Work Education Reporter*, Vol. 20, September/October 1972, pp. 43–47.

11. *Ibid.*

12. Jay Haley, *Problem Solving Therapy*, San Francisco, Jossey Bass Publishers, 1976.

13. Carlton E. Munson, "Professional Autonomy and Social Work Supervision," *Journal of Education for Social Work*, Vol. 12, No. 3, Fall 1976, pp. 95–102.

14. Frances H. Scherz, "A Concept of Supervision Based on Definitions of Job Responsibility," *Social Casework*, Vol. 39, October 1958, pp. 436–437.

15. Epstein, *op. cit.*

16. Louise Frey, Eunice Shatz, and Edna-Ann Katz, "Continuing Education—Teaching Staff to Teach," *Social Casework*, Vol. 55, June 1974, pp. 364–365.

17. J.G. Whitaker, "The Issue of Mandatory Continuing Education," *Nursing Clinics of North America*, Vol. 9, September 1974, pp. 472–478.

18. Barbara Berkman, and Helen Rehr, *Clients of Medical Social Workers: Satisfaction with Social Services*, Division of Social Work, Mount Sinai School of Medicine, City University of New York, 1974, mimeographed report.

19. David M. Kaplan, "The Montana Experience: Practice Perspectives," *Competency Based Education for Social Work*, edited by Morton Arkava and E. Clifford Brennen, New York, Council on Social Work Education, 1976, pp. 156–162.

9

Social Work Education for Professional Accountability: The Hunter College School of Social Work and Mount Sinai School of Medicine Consortium

PHYLLIS CAROFF
AND MARILYN WILSON

The objective of this chapter is to document the experience to date of the Hunter College School of Social Work and the Mount Sinai Division of Social Work, Mount Sinai School of Medicine, in collaboratively designing and implementing a two-year Consortium curriculum to educate master's level social work students for existing and emerging roles in health care systems, with particular emphasis on self-directed accountable practice. This experience demonstrates that commitment and readiness to address program design in the context of mutually held objectives is a means to obviate unproductive debate about the relative contributions of practice and academia toward achieving professional competence.

Relevant Background

The establishment of the Mount Sinai School of Medicine and its affiliation with the City University of New York, and the Medical School's inclusion of the Division of Social Work as an essential component of the Department of Community Medicine, gave impetus to the identification and development of practice bases for systematic efforts and evaluation of new ways to educate social workers for expanding roles in markedly different patterns of service delivery. A student unit established in the Mount Sinai Department of Social Work Services in 1970 served as a pilot project for the preliminary design of a field curriculum. This experience was the foundation for the development of the Hunter School of Social Work–Mount Sinai School of Medicine Consortium.

The decision of the Hunter College School of Social Work, in 1972, to develop its curriculum along modular lines, based on a concept of human needs as its organizing rubric, provided a needed structural arrangement within the school to consider what was being learned from the Mount Sinai experience and to evaluate its relevance for the education of all students in health agencies. The Social Health Module, the organizational designation for the cohort of campus faculty, field agencies, and students in the health area (approximately one-third of the total student body) was charged to develop a curriculum which identified core knowledge for all social work students as well as that required for competent social work practice in health. The creation of a school-agency curriculum committee as the major curriculum development body for the module reflected the school's acceptance of the need for the academic-practice partnership in the education of social work students, and the agencies' readiness to contribute their scarce resources to this endeavor.[1]

The receipt of an NIMH grant in Summer 1975 marked the beginning of the Consortium. While only partially funding the ideal design, the grant did allow for the start of its implementation.[2] Clearly, the decision to fund the project reflected the interest of NIMH in the affiliated relationship between the School of Social Work and the Mount Sinai Complex, as such relationship facilitated the collaborative design of the curriculum. The Consortium perceived school and agency as an educational unit, with content being taught on multiple campuses as appropriate to objectives and the resources available for their achievement.

Rationale and Objectives
for the Consortium

A primary motivation for this educational endeavor was the concern of school and agency about the educational product and the degree of success or failure to educate adequately as required for professional practice in a rapidly changing delivery system in health. More specifically, the authors perceived that entry-level social work health professionals would of necessity have to be self-directed; accountable to the profession, to clients, and to the community; perceive themselves as full partners in an inter-professional endeavor called health care; and have sufficiently diverse educational experience to develop a system of inquiry and evaluation.

It was agreed that the total student education had to be more closely modelled on what would be demanded in creative professional performance, that traditional learning/teaching methods did not seem to socialize students adequately for the demands of entry-level professional work in the social health arena.

The Consortium in Operation

This section describes the Consortium's current operation to facilitate its objectives. Included are the roles and tasks of the educators participating in the project; the design of the educational activity, including the rationale for its planning; the contribution of Consortium faculty to curriculum development in both class and field; and initial efforts at evaluation.

The institutional partnership consists of the Hunter College School of Social Work and three affiliated institutions in the Mount Sinai School of Medicine: Beth Israel Hospital, The Hospital for Joint Diseases, and The Mount Sinai Hospital.

The Educational Corps

The underlying premise of the core design is to transmit knowledge through use of multiple teachers as role models and through exposure to a variety of learning experiences, in order to facilitate the development of a more self-directed, accountable practitioner. Therefore, preceptors selected from the practice staff of the social work services departments of the Consortium's teaching hospitals became the models for service delivery for the students. Two full-time faculty members, one from the Division of Social Work and one appointed from the Hunter College School of Social Work, provide educational coordination of the total student experience. These coordinators, along with preceptors, share responsibilities for the field work program and constitute the Educational Corps.

The leadership and administrative responsibilities of the

educational coordinators are to identify and develop educational resources, advise on the number and kind of student those resources can absorb, select the students, and maintain liaison with faculty members of the Division of Social Work whose institutions provide the practicum. The coordinators also have primary responsibility for implementing educational objectives through the program design. In addition, they provide direction and consultation for preceptors in the educational role, evaluate the progress of the program with the project director, and make recommendations to the project's educational advisory committee: the administrators of the institutions involved, the project director, and selected faculty. The coordinators also teach students directly in both individual and group sessions. (The use of the group will be discussed later in this chapter.)

Individual meetings with students provide the occasion to determine learning opportunities and assignments appropriate to individual student needs, abilities, interests, and potentials, and to enhance integration of the total experience by identifying the individual student's learning patterns, progression in learning, and level of performance. A major role of the coordinators is to make explicit and work to alleviate specific learning difficulties. Coordinators are responsible for the overall evaluation of the student's performance, including the ability to use the totality of learning/teaching experiences.

The preceptors in the Educational Corps have direct teaching responsibility within the time frame of students' assignment to their particular service. Each preceptor teaches the specific social work role and practice in his service area, the characteristics of the patient population served, the common bio/psycho/social needs of this population, the health care delivery system, the role and function of members of other health disciplines within the system, the resources available to meet the needs of the population, and the accountability measures, particularly recording for professional and service purposes.

Such teaching is primarily didactic and emphasizes the "how-to" of practice. The preceptor facilitates the student's entry into the service area and arranges opportunities for the student to learn from the expertise of other disciplines. The preceptor serves as a role model, providing frequent planned observation of his or her own activity with clients, in interprofessional collaboration, and in the management of systems. Thus, the openness of the preceptor to expose his own practice as the student's learning model before assuming a similar responsibility serves to prepare the student for professional accountability in peer review, as well as in other accountability measures. The preceptor also carries an evaluative responsibility for the students, assigned within written guidelines that define the particular dimensions for which the preceptor, in this role, is responsible.

Design for Student Learning

To implement the educational objectives, students are exposed, within the health care system, to a variety of experiences which encompass both medical and psychiatric services along a continuum of preventive through rehabilitative care. On both in- and outpatient units, students observe the delivery of direct services to varied patient populations, age range from infancy to old age; of diverse economic and sociocultural backgrounds; with medical and psychiatric illness, acute, chronic, and terminal; in case problems necessitating both planned long- and short-term treatment and crisis intervention, using individual, group, and family treatment modalities. Practice is collaborative, both intra- and interprofessional, involving other health care professions and paraprofessionals. Experiences in health education and prevention are provided through practice in adolescent programs and family planning clinics. Since the institutions are located in geographic areas serving large ethnic and minority populations who are also poor, student learning has required the development of knowledge, attitudes, and skills which increase the possibility that these groups will receive quality care.

Placement of students in specific service areas integrates them into the system and demonstrates that social work practice in health is an intra- and interprofessional endeavor. A system of inquiry emphasizes for the student the essential content areas to be learned for quality practice and provides a framework which aids the transfer of learning to any health care system within which the student might practice in the future. This content encompasses particular disease and illness entities; the social health needs of population groups, and the resources, including social work services, available to meet these needs; the delivery system and the nature of the intra- and interprofessional collaboration within the system. Policy issues, as these may enhance or inhibit client access to the service, its availability, and acceptability, are stressed, providing the basis for evaluation.

The project design calls for initial assignment of every student to deliver services in more than one service area, thereby immediately involving the student with two preceptors. Rotation to additional services is possible within the academic year, with mini-assignments to broaden the learning experience. Among the mini-assignments are opportunities to observe a designated area of practice, participation on institutional board committees, and attendance at community board meetings, to heighten the student's perception of the institution's role as part of the larger health care delivery system. Efforts are made to design assignments in conjunction with classroom requirements, to reinforce the class-field collaboration. Students partcipate in their educational planning with teachers on the basis of their learning needs.

On Preparing for Self-Directed Accountable Practice

This section highlights attempts to implement the project objectives in the practicum, emphasizing enhancement of the student's self-directedness as a learner and sense of accountability not only to the institution but to the consumer, the profession, and the community. While such emphasis pervades the educational design, the authors call attention to certain experiences which appeared to have critical impact.

The project values and encourages free exchange of ideas. This expectation is communicated, through structural arrangements and by the mentors, that students become more independent as learners and increasingly assume the responsibility of identifying what they need to know and from whom this can be obtained, thus accelerating progress toward self-directed activity. In addition to individual contacts with coordinators and preceptors, students are required to share their decision making with their teachers and peers in both formal and informal groups and to evaluate their own activity, creating an attitude which prepares them for professional peer review. Furthermore, this experience enables more cogent communication and documentation of social work practice to other professionals.

The group learning format was significantly expanded to make certain that all students were: (1) aware of the principles underlying practice; (2) learning to organize material for presentation; (3) learning to expose and share their own practice, strengths, and weaknesses; (4) beginning to experience the meaning of consultation and to be constructively critical of each other.

The Consortium educators identified content areas needing special emphasis in the field practicum to achieve Consortium objectives. Review of existing classroom curricula had suggested that this designated content was insufficiently covered. The number of students and the resources available within the Consortium made possible mini-courses in the field with didactic emphasis, required readings, and an assignment. This experiment provided a pilot study for testing the organization and sequencing of such content for potential inclusion in the school's health module curriculum. The first areas developed in the mini-course format included: collaboration, sociocultural factors as these affect access to and use of medical care, and attention to the requirements for audit and peer review. As this is written, health module faculty have begun to integrate the conceptualized teaching around collaboration, developed in the Consortium, into the overall curriculum for health students. Research faculty are in addition considering how preparation for mandated accountability measures in health can be integrated into the research curriculum.[3]

It remains to be seen to what extent the classroom, with its range and variety of demands, can or should teach the specific content needed for the specialized demands of health practice. It may be that the field practicum must take more responsibility for didactic teaching of such content in the students' overall education. If this is so, then the school and agency institutions will have to examine how the responsibilities are to be shared, including the issue of granting credit beyond that given to field instruction.

Recording—An Educational Tool for the Development of
Practice Skill and the Assurance of Accountability

The health professions' demand that they become increasingly accountable through professional audits and peer review has forced the Consortium's attention to conceptualizing more clearly how the "record" attests to evidence of service and quality practice. Included in any definition of quality practice is the requirement of accountability to clients, to the profession, and to the community, including the service agency and its funding sources. From the beginning, students must meet a variety of recording demands within the guidelines and practice of the particular institution; one of their more difficult initial tasks is to conceptualize activity at a time that they are beginning learners, unsure of their own practice.

Formerly, the process record was thought to be the most desirable format to teach practice. The Consortium has tested the potential of a variety of recording mechanisms to facilitate this teaching and learning. Heavy emphasis on the process record has not provided the structure to foster clarity about (1) purpose, (2) responsibility to make explicit actions which had produced desired movement and those which had failed, (3) evaluation of treatment plans and goals to be pursued or modified in relation to additional data, and (4) relevant collaborative activity. In the Consortium, process is used initially for student and educational coordinator to assess the student's practice level and determine learning needs. Beyond beginnings, tape recordings and audiovisual aids are introduced along with selective use of process to help students with their individualized learning. An important new mechanism to facilitate recording for the patient's chart and enhance practice skill has been developed, in the form of an interviewing guide. This guide emphasizes purposeful practice by requiring the statement of objectives for each interview, the identification of major themes, the evaluation of interview accomplishment (including student and client satisfaction), and the plan for next steps (including collaborative activity). A section of the guide calls for selected student-client interactions to focus on particularly significant content, either to deepen understanding of the client and his problem or to clarify areas of difficulty in the student-client exchange. Thus, proper use of this guide provides a format for encouraging early conceptualization of practice, material for learning skill in interviewing, and identifying additional areas for work. It bridges the educational need for some detailing to learn skill in depth as well as in the professional clarity required to enhance practice and accountability demands, as in chart recording. (See Exhibit 19.)

The guide has been tested with students in the Consortium. Initially, they found its use more difficult than traditional process recording, but they agreed that it succeeded in promoting more self-direction and independence in thinking about the needs of the client and their interventions in meeting these needs. The interest of other health settings in testing this guide by introducing it to other field teachers in the Social Health Module provided an opportunity for its evaluation by a larger number of students and teachers.

Special Assignment Emphases

Historically, the need for social work services in health has too often been defined and initiated by other professions within the system, primarily through referral. The Consortium's belief that social work input is intrinsic to the bio-psycho-social concept of diagnosis and treatment planning for patients and families provides the rationale for assigning students to services requiring high social risk screening or introducing them to the skills needed to enter a service system where the social work contribution has not been fully experienced. These activities, plus efforts at conjoint education, can demonstrate social work's role in interprofessional health care and are further elaborated in this section.

For example, high social risk screenings of inpatient units, part of the social work department's involvement in mandated utilization review, provide the mechanism through which social work students enter case situations early to assure continuity of care. Here, they learn criteria for the identification of patients at risk, and the importance of collaborative input from other health professionals to achieve mutual agreement with patient and family for services during the period of hospitalization and post-hospitalization, where needed. This experience promotes stronger identification for the students with the importance of social work in the health care system, and more clarity regarding social work's role. All of this develops a more confident social work attitude toward other professionals within the system.

Program development as a learning task has been identified as having particular potential to foster creativity and reinforce knowledge of major content areas central to effective and efficient service. Such development further emphasizes, for students, awareness of the relationship of social work services to the purposes for which clients come to the institution. Therefore students were assigned to a speciality clinic, in which there was minimal social work service, to demonstrate and evaluate the extent of the need for social work. This required that the student understand: (1) the extant system; (2) the nature, cause, and course of the particular illness and its medical treatment; (3) the criteria for identifying patients at risk; and (4) the setting of priorities for social work intervention, including the differential use of social work manpower to maximize the effectiveness of limited resources. The experience demonstrated the processes required which, in fact, supported the crucial place of interprofessional collaboration in assessing need and in determining and evaluating how such need was to be met in this clinic. After the program development experience, a set of working guidelines and criteria for social work function on that service were developed. The principles underlying the guidelines were considered applicable for social work entry into other service areas.

The objectives of the Department of Community Medicine —to enhance physicians' knowledge and appreciation of the interplay of social, psychological, and environmental factors in determining health status and potential for social functioning—are consonant with those of social work education. Therefore, a conjoint social work and medical student educational experience was developed in the second year medical school course, "Determinants of Family Health." This experiment is based on the hypothesis that conjoint learning, which emphasizes the primary expertise of each professional as well as the essential need for interprofessional work, is desirable for all professional health students. Early socialization to a conjoint experience is assumed to improve future collaborative practice. The design of the course, which called for conjoint assessment of the health needs of a family, included guidelines on how to approach this question, plus small group discussion with interprofessional faculty. While the course left many unanswered questions, it did serve to demonstrate that interprofessional learning can be implemented on a student level even though students are in the process of developing their own identity and role clarity. The fact that the students are not yet socialized to a set role can bring more flexibility to their learning situation than may be found among practicing professionals who are meeting social health needs.[4] Developing more interprofessional educational opportunities to enhance future professional practice is an area in which Consortium educators plan further work.

Analysis of the examples presented, which emphasize the interprofessional nature of health care and review the Consortium's major teaching emphases for direct practice, highlight the hand-in-glove relationship of knowledge and skill required for quality practice and for accountability. Furthermore, valuing collaborative endeavors as intrinsic to quality practice reinforces, for students, recognition of the professions' common concerns about the social and emotional impact of illness and the problems in patients' compliance with medical treatment. It is anticipated that these experiences will reinforce the educational position that accountable professional practice for social workers in health care is not a solo practice; it requires relevant collaboration with other professionals for assessment, for the achievement of mutual agreement with patients and families, for treatment planning, implementation, and evaluation of its quality care. If, indeed, the students' socialization to the profession has a lasting effect on future professional practice, then it may be expected that the future health practitioner will reflect this approach to service delivery in his work in health systems.

Educational Processes Supporting Systematic Evaluation

The obligation to evaluate one's practice has been built into the educational design of the Consortium. Emphasis on the evaluation of performance on a case-by-case basis has always been part of social work education; in this project, also, preparation of students for professional peer review reflects this level of accountability. However, a gap in student education exists: helping the student to experience his work as part of the system's accountability to the community served, including the funding sources. Statistics have been used dynamically to underscore students' activity in relation to normative expectations, including the importance of the selective use of time with respect to educational and service priorities and the patterning of work. Availability of measures to study the student's performance over time moves him or her toward an internalization of accountability as a professional. The use of student statistics by the educational coordinators and preceptors, to teach the importance of quantifying activity to document social work services in the larger institution, provides the opportunity to sensitize students to the costs of service, reimbursement mechanisms, and the legislative problems therein. Of particular importance is the power of cumulative statistics to define the utilization of service by given populations. This enables the student to consider, on the basis of the data, how needs are met or remain unmet, and fosters sensitivity to issues of access, availability, and acceptability of service.

Student participation in a pilot experiment is especially important for utilizing a standardized research mechanism. This research tool is designed to test the impact of the educational design on one aspect of student performance; namely, the process of problem identification and the establishment of mutual agreement with patients and families in relation to intervention and outcome. Outcome is defined by change in problem situation, measure of client and student satisfaction with results, and the relationship of these judgments to resource availability. With respect to mutual agreement, the research instrument can, potentially, identify the extent of the participation by significant others, professional and family, and the use of community resources. A prior, small pilot effort confirmed the viability of this instrument to test student progress along the dimensions studied, within the time frame of the education. The authors view this experience as fostering accountability to the clients because the instrument judges whether or not problem situations have changed and why, and heightens student consciousness about the importance of a clear focus on both student and client satisfaction. Thus, the student also develops a more sensitized perception of professional accountability. The necessity for students to document activity cumulatively can foster the study of cases in aggregates, by service, problem definition, and so forth, as these relate to outcome. This study provides an opportunity to experience the intent of audit, i.e., self- and agency inquiry, and also educates the educators concerning gaps in teaching and learning.

As of this writing, two additional student-faculty projects have been completed; these show the necessity for systematic evaluation as a means to effect change responsibly. The first is a student study, with preceptor assistance, to identify communication patterns, gaps, and problems within the educational corps and student cohort. The second is a student survey designed to tap student satisfaction with the educational experience and to obtain student input for future modification. These two studies have brought about changes in the project design and its implementation, resulting in a significantly more productive start to this third year of the project.

Summary

This chapter has described the background and rationale for the Consortium project, its objectives, its organization and structure, the learning/teaching design, and specific examples of its implementation as these relate to educational preparation for self-directed accountable professional practice.

At present, the authors' commitment to the concept of Consortium is based on a number of assumptions and some observable behavioral changes in students, in field teachers, and in agency staff, as a result of the Consortium's presence. The Consortium has just begun the systematic study required to demonstrate that this design does indeed better prepare students for the demands of health practice. In this third year of the project, all students' direct service activity with individuals and families will be included in the problem classification study. The next step has been projected as a comparison of the Consortium students' performance with that of health module students in other health settings, as measured by this instrument. If adequate funding is secured, a follow-up of graduates of the Consortium, compared with a similar group of recent graduates from other schools working in health, would serve to affirm or deny the impact of this educational project. The authors are cognizant of their accountability in educating for the profession, which includes awareness of the concepts of cost effectiveness and cost benefit.

This chapter may encourage other institutions educating

master's level social work students to realize the desirability of finding ways to work collaboratively toward commonly held objectives. The fundamental requirement is that school and agency be open to examining their own ways of operating, and that they seek together to determine if their educational programming prepares beginning workers for the challenges of rapidly changing health practice with its emphasis on professional accountability. Clearly, none of the efforts described would have been possible without a readiness to move from traditionally held prerogatives and accept the probable necessity to give up overworked concern about autonomy.

References

1. For explication of the rationale underlying the curriculum reorganization of the Hunter College School of Social Work and the school agency collaborative process in developing curriculum, see: Phyllis Caroff, and Elinor Stevens, "School-Agency Collaboration in Curriculum Development for Social Work in Health," presented at the 22nd Annual Program Meeting, Council on Social Work Education, Philadelphia, March 1976. Also see Phyllis Caroff, "A Study of School-Agency Collaboration in Social Work in Health Curriculum Building," *Social Work in Health Care,* Vol. 2, No. 3, Spring 1977, pp. 329–339.

For a fuller description of the collaborative development of a course curriculum offering, a precursor of the Consortium, see Mildred Mailick, "Education and Practice, An Intra Professional Collaborative Venture," presented at the 22nd Annual Program Meeting, Council on Social Work Education, Philadelphia, March 1976.

2. For explication of the full design, see Phyllis Caroff, and Ruth Fizdale, "Hunter College School of Social Work–Mount Sinai School of Medicine Consortium," memorandum to the Executive Planning Committee, Hunter College School of Social Work–Mt. Sinai School of Medicine Consortium (unpublished), April 1976.

3. For information about the experience of one school of social work in confronting this demand, see Helen Reinherz, et al., "Training in Accountability: A Social Work Mandate," *Health and Social Work,* Vol. 2, No. 2, May 1977, pp. 43–56.

4. Marilyn Wilson, and George Jackson, "Interprofessional Education: Learning Together," presented at the 22nd Annual Program Meeting, Council on Social Work Education, Philadelphia, March 1976.

10

The Professional Staff Views
Accountability

DOROTHY TOPPER, JOAN ZOFNASS,
ELLEN SMITH, AND JANE PARSONS

The reports in this chapter are based on the staff's accounts of some of their experiences while participating in the process of developing and refining standards and methods of accountability. Mrs. Topper's statement discusses the application of high-risk screening criteria; Miss Zofnass describes the influence of a contracting and outcome oriented practice. Ms. Smith and Mrs. Parsons describe the experience of a group of twelve social workers, with five or more years of postgraduate experience, meeting weekly over a period of several months. The purpose of this group was to examine its practice in accordance with criteria for the self-directed worker, and then to determine for each social worker areas for ongoing learning and development.

Early Case-finding and Intervention[1]

In translating the intent of PSRO for social work services in an acute care hospital, the Department has set up a peer review system, charged with the development of standards, norms, and criteria which social work as a discipline will use to evaluate its own practice. To this end, and in line with the utilization and review legislation, staff has addressed itself to the issue of early case-finding and intervention, based on identification of high risk medical/social factors as profile on pre-admission screenings. The intent of such interventions is:

    a. To involve the social worker at the onset of hospitalization when the patient is struggling with the problems and concerns of leaving home and having to adjust, at the same time, to the routines and procedures of hospitalization (in short, the very process of becoming a patient, while retaining a sense of self)

b. Where indicated, to assist the patient in coping with the effect of his illness/prognosis and its implications for his future level of functioning

Because the social worker has more time, via early intervention, in which to work with the patient/family and their support system, an ongoing collaborative health care structure can be built into the pre-admission, admission, and post-hospital planning process. Early intervention also affords the social worker time to work with the total continuum of diagnosis-treatment within an expanded concept of discharge planning. Issues and questions centering on illness and post-hospital planning options can then be verbalized and realistically explored with the patient, his family, and the health care staff. Since ultimate responsibility for establishing appropriate priorities for early intervention lies with the social worker, at this point it is necessary to consider areas of difficulty which must be resolved in order to make the system a more effective one. For example, social workers need to feel more comfortable with the new outreach role, which entails teaching-learning. The first few interviews present a particular responsibility: helping patient/family and the worker to determine whether or not future casework services are needed. How the social worker initially appears to the patient/family depends largely upon how clearly the worker understands what to look for, and, in keeping with PSRO regulations, how effectively that can be entered into the medical chart. In short, this marks the beginning of an assessment of those social, psychological, and medical factors which affect the patient and his family's ability to cope with the crisis of illness and the disruption of their previous life style. How to recognize the patient and his family's unarticulated needs, and how to enable clients to recognize and verbalize those needs so that they can be worked on in a planned, collaborative effort is an area which tests all the social worker's skill.

One other area of concern is the need to refine the identification of high social risk diagnosis and how certain illnesses affect social functioning. Although other referral sources provide equally legitimate reasons for intervention, a major merit of the new intake procedure is that it allows a shift from a more passive to a more active, independent role in case-finding, assessment, and intervention. This area of expertise is the Department's contribution to the total collaborative health care effort on behalf of the patient.

Contracting, Problem-Outcome, and Audits[2]

In accordance with the social worker's prevailing need to reassess what his or her tasks are, the reason for them, and whether they are worth doing, the profession faces the fact that such questions are not nearly so ridiculous as they may, at first, sound. A professional group, to insure its own position, must be able readily to identify what its function is and insure that this knowledge is also well understood by the consumer. Once the social worker and the consumer both know what can be done, then the worker can decide whether it makes sense to offer a service and the consumer can decide whether or not to participate.

Assuming for the moment that the two, consumer and professional, have agreed upon a plan and proceed with it, it seems only natural to check the results and assess the progress. It is mandatory that the professional validate the intervention as a professional, for the consumer and for the employer. If social workers can systematically study the who, why, and how, they can respond directly, intelligently, and non-defensively to questions raised as to their profession's worth and justifiability. First steps in this direction have, fortunately, already begun.

In the adult inpatient medical/surgical units, the quality assurance study of May through September 1975 was an initial step in PSRO. The study had a variety of purposes and some serendipitous outcomes. At the onset of intervention, the initial assessment form was completed by checking off reasons for referral as identified by referral source and the social problems identified by the social worker. The study developed an accountability mechanism by focusing on the terms of the contract and the results achieved. Furthermore, the study offered an overview of social problems perceived by others in the health care system and permitted correlation between social work-identified problems, contracts agreed upon, and the outcome of those contracts. It correlated professional satisfaction in relation to consumer satisfaction and offered an accounting of services given.

While the intricacies of the study must be left to statisticians to decipher, practitioners can begin to examine the implications and results of auditing their own work. For instance, just by having to complete the Berkman-Rehr questionnaire for each new patient interviewed after May 1, the author had immediately to focus her thinking on what, precisely, she was doing. Once her own thoughts had become more specific, she could convey to the consumer more articulately what she could offer. No longer did she feel comfortable writing a global chart note of the intervention—"Will work with patient on supportive basis," but instead she began to spell out specific issues which she and the patient *together* had decided to work on, such as "Contracted with patient to work on feelings of isolation aroused by hospitalization," or "Agreed to explore with patient and family the growing difficulties patient's chronic illness have placed on all family members." If the worker is not as global, neither is the consumer, and the two can more readily head toward the contracted goals. If the worker can clarify the purpose of intervention and the success at outcome, and the consumer too can pinpoint the intervention and value, together with physicians, administrators, and others, then social workers can continue to validate the social work role.

To attain such valid justification for social work, workers must therefore question themselves. What makes them competent? How is competence defined? Do the number of interviews affect outcome? Can the mean number of interviews based on contract established be estimated? What happens in the case of sequential goals? When are workers least able to complete a contract? Who are the consumers? What does it really mean when both worker and consumer identify a primary contract and a positive resolution? What are the effects of good collaboration with the interdisciplinary team? How can work of poor quality be more easily identified?

A critical examination of social work makes possible identification of its strengths and weaknesses and a beginning at resolving specific problem areas. Without such auditing, it is not only impossible to expand qualitatively, but the lack encourages an unscientific, unsound, unjustified professional position.

As social workers become more conscious of their tools, how these can best be used, what the results will be and are, then they gain more control of their own future, and are less in the hands of others' allocation. The implications of auditing, of critical self-assessment, the author believes, are the difference between tenuous existence as an ancillary, adjunct to a host system, versus existence as a viable necessary profession.

Self-Directedness and Peer Review: Beginnings and Values[3]

At the first two meetings, the statement of expectations for experienced professional practice was shared with the group. (This group consisted of twelve workers with five or more years' experience, whose charge was to develop criteria for identifying the self-directed worker.) In addition, the group was to meet regularly for the purpose of continued learning. These meetings were viewed as an alternative to traditional supervision in the hope that from them would develop a broader-based reservoir of supervisory and educational modalities. The group felt they needed to meet with one another as a first step, to begin the process and to determine their needs.

From June through October, 1974, the following steps were taken: (1) A survey of the workers revealed that only one of the twelve reviewed had weekly supervision. Many felt that their learning needs were being met via group supervision, seminars, and so on; that traditional supervision for advanced workers was limiting and infantilizing. In addition, each worker drew up a list of learning needs. (2) A proposal for continuing professional growth of experienced workers was drawn up and included the following:

    a. The worker, when starting a new experience, should be expected to choose from one of the following as a modality of learning:
        i.   Group supervision
       ii. Individual supervision
     iii. Attendance at seminars
      iv. Consultation with hospital staff
       v. Training situation or consultation outside hospital
    b. After five years' experience the worker, in order to enhance professional growth, should have a teaching or supervisory experience. If the worker has an interest in

administration or research, this opportunity should be offered in place of or together with the above-mentioned teaching opportunity. This greater responsibility will enhance further growth and enable the worker to contribute more effectively to departmental goals.

(3) As a result of getting to know one another through examining each other's work, the group discovered that each had one or more areas of expertise. Some consciousness raising was necessary to help workers validate for themselves the quality of their skills in particular areas; this was done by means of an experience bank, which each worker drew up and shared with the group. Then an experience bank for the whole group was compiled, with the purpose of identifying which workers were available for consultation in specific areas of their experience. This list was forwarded to administration.

In November, the group returned to considering the list of criteria for a self-directed worker. Thirteen criteria were identified (see Exhibit 20) and, as the group looked at the criteria, they tried to arrive at a time span in which this could and should be achieved. Five years of practice was agreed on as a reasonable expectation, with the recognition that some workers will achieve this level of practice in fewer years and others will need longer, that a worker with advanced skills may be less skilled in a particular new treatment modality, that the development of skills may be uneven, and that there will be greater strength in certain areas than in others.

In December, the group met with Dr. Rehr on the issue of accountability. As a result of this meeting, the group appreciated the importance of establishing an accountability mechanism. A case load review outline, devised to analyze the group's case loads, took the following form:

1. Patient's name
2. Demographic data
3. Length of time seen
4. Frequency of appointments
5. Presenting problem from the point of view of the referral source, the patient, and the worker
6. Diagnosis and severity
7. Goals

8. Intervention—type of service given
9. Collaboration
10. Outcome
    a. Was goal achieved?
    b. What changes occurred?
    Or—Current status vis-à-vis goals
11. Was patient satisfied? Client's view of outcome
12. Date of last chart notation
13. Hours spent on case
14. Contract

The group devised a plan to use the review instrument to study every fifth case on their November 1974 printouts. They agreed to discuss trends identified as a result of considering their work from these perspectives and agreed to choose a worker from a service other than their own to look over each other's reviews in terms of trends perceived. The group's patients were asked why they thought they were coming to see the social workers and whether or not they were satisfied with the service they were receiving.

In order to study each worker's review, the group divided in two, in early February. Both groups functioned simultaneously: each worker presented her case review sheet and identified the practice trends and issues which had become apparent as a result of the review. The groups then focused on specific areas which were identified; e.g., management of the chronically ill psychiatric patient; what to do when the worker's view of the presenting problem is different from the patient's; how the worker allies herself with the patient when the institution's goals are different from the patient's goals. The case load reviews continued into June 1975.

The case load review provided an enriching experience for all the group, who saw the kind of work done on other services and gained a healthy respect for each other's practice skills. It was gratifying to see that each worker evaluated his or her cases thoroughly and had a sound knowledge of the dynamics of human behavior. It also became apparent that the group undervalued and oversimplified their work, which was more skilled and complex in practice than the description on paper.

Of greatest importance was that the group learned to look

at cases in a different way: consciously to value the notion of contract, the setting up of an agreement between worker and patient in which both are totally clear about what they are going to work on together. By comparing previously set goals with the presenting problem, the group began to see that goals were often too general and overambitious; setting global goals often aroused dissatisfaction with the work. By setting more specific and appropriate goals for each case, the group learned to partialize in terms of what problems could be tackled first and to set sequential goals in order to help patients solve their problems. Redefining goals led to the discovery that the outcome was often more successful than originally perceived. Viewing cases in this way led to the further realization that it could easily be determined if outcomes were successful or not. These discoveries were crucial. They moved the group to support structural approaches in assessing the work of the individual practitioner and in auditing the general delivery of care, and to regard their own investment in peer review and audit as components of professional accountability.

References

[1] Based on a report prepared by Dorothy Topper, social worker at The Mount Sinai Hospital, and presented at the Department's staff meeting, April 21, 1976.

[2] Based on a report prepared by Joan Zofnass, social worker at The Mount Sinai Hospital and presented at the Department's staff meeting, April 21, 1976.

[3] Based on a report, dated July 1975, summarizing experienced worker group meetings, June 1974–June 1975, prepared by Ellen Smith and Jane Parsons.

11

Looking to the Future*

HELEN REHR

To be professional is to be accountable, to be answerable to someone or to some group, to possess full and complete information upon which decisions can be made, decisions which are judgments relating to a program, a population, or a patient and his family. In professional terms accountability is the capacity and capability to assume responsibility for those acts and behaviors undertaken to achieve the objectives determined. Professional acts are performed as a part of "social contract," the profession's contract with society, which affords the profession relative autonomy and self-regulation in the conduct of its affairs; in return, society expects the profession to safeguard the public trust by responsible behavior and practice that shows both quality and efficiency. To fulfill its "social contract" is the hallmark of a mature profession. A key characteristic of a profession is that it sets standards for its members' practice. Another is that it monitors professional services, correcting where necessary and, in general, advancing the quality of all.

Professional accountability, in the final analysis, is to the client system. How this accountability is translated into the delivery of quality services is the key determinant, lodged in the professional himself. To be qualified and accountable, the professional must have much available to him: knowledge, skills, values, and ethical attitudes and behaviors. He must know costs and management, the meaning of availability and accessibility, and understand implementation of quality and quantity assurance. Resources for practice must be available to him. All of this implies the availability of good data, the knowledge to assess them, and the freedom to use the informed results within the rules and regulations set by the public and other regulatory bodies, while seeking to change these, if necessary. Quality information and its

*Several of these opinions have been stated in earlier articles. However, these have been updated in the light of more recent studies and experiences.

sound utilization are the foundations in the conduct of accountability. However, to assume this professional stance requires socialization into the profession, into its "social contract," and into its obligation "pro bono publico." For social work this is more than a commitment to the economically deprived; it is a commitment to the public, in general, who can benefit from social work services. In assuming professional accountability, the profession must free itself of the constraints and restrictions, unnecessarily imposed by the social system, and commit itself to professional values. This change calls for new organizational relationships between professional staff and administrators and for new responsibilities and expectations from each. A number of assumptions underlie the assessment of quality care. These are:

1. "Good" care is recognizable.
2. Decisions regarding the appropriateness of the service are subjective and value-laden.
3. Experts can agree, in general, on standards for "good" care.
4. "Good" care can be specified by defined elements, which can be rated.
5. The definition of "good" care is predicated on present knowledge, opinions, and values.

Many problems beset the process of quality assurance. At what, when, at whom, where, and even how to look are only a few of the questions facing each profession or provider. Assessment of the quality of care is a complex issue, involving many factors interactive with clinical management. Included in the process of care are the key components of judgment and decision making which touch critically on quality and outcome, which as yet are not measurable, and which, by and large, are unlisted among the criteria of most assessment inventories. All practitioners are reassured that there is still so little known that no universal or uniform prescription for giving "good" care impends. Likelihood of a common practice orientation is also most improbable in spite of computers and projected data banks. However, we cannot stop the process because we have not reached the perfect evaluation state. We must proceed with the crude instruments we have, improving and advancing as we go. We have already learned much and know how much more is to be learned.

New Administrative Directions

Administrators of social work departments must find their way into the overall planning programs of their institutions. They and professional social workers increasingly will discover themselves on utilization review committees, patient care committees, and audit reviewing bodies. Utilization committees are responsible for developing policies that affect medical care delivery and for the social determinants affecting such care. It falls to the medical institution to assess appropriate utilization of its resources. Social work, as one of the hospital's services and in its frequent role of coordinator of many services, must be available to all patients and to their families, must thus assume responsibility for offering services to those patients who need them, and to motivate them to use these services. Although regulations mandate a place on the utilization review committee for social work, social work must assume and sustain an active role. It is therefore essential that every hospital, through its social work department, institutionalize a written plan to insure the recognition of those patients requiring assistance, so that social work services can be provided.

A member of a utilization review committee must expect to have a place on the audit committee, whatever form that takes. Social work is expected to evaluate its own services and then to contribute to intraprofessional audits. In any event, the process of evaluation calls for recommendations to deal with uncovered problems in the delivery of care. Continued education is expected to be available to maintain and secure better staff practice. The means are already available for quality assurance and can be employed by one-member qualified departments as well as by multi-member professional departments. The intent of quality assurance is to govern every hospital department, small or large, by standards; social work standards will be a component of institutional (and provider) accreditation by regulatory bodies in order to safeguard the services given to patients.

Early Case-finding, Guaranteed Access, and Quality Discharge Planning

The utilization review system deems social work the means by which individuals and families who enter a medical care system and who are at high social risk can secure needed social services as early as possible. Social work must initiate its own case-finding in order to assure access to its services.

Social work can no longer wait for referrals. These have been demonstrated to be late in the stay, usually in the third or fourth quarter of hospitalization, or when prescribed ambulatory care has resulted in missed appointments or in dropouts. At present, there are very few systematic ways to reach patients, other than by referral. Patients and their families with social problems related to illness or to hospitalization must be found early in order to comply with utilization review, expectations of predicted length of stay, and, shortly, to meet ambulatory care requirements as well. Doctors are responsible for the majority of those patients who enter a social work system, followed by patients who themselves seek assistance. In either instance, the patient reaches social services late in the caring pattern. The explanation for late referrals is ascribed to physicians' involvement in diagnostic work-ups, and to patients' involvement with the illness and the hospitalization. Such concentration tends to defer thinking of post-hospital planning until a later time in the hospital stay. In all probability, under these belated approaches to social factors, many patients and their families with social problems do not reach social services at all. It is therefore essential that social work reach patients and families in need, irrespective of the preoccupations of physician and patient.

Every department will need to undertake its own means to high social risk screening to uncover social problems related to the medical condition. Other indicators of vulnerability, in addition to predicted long stay, should be utilized, at admission or in pre-admission, if possible. Uncovering "high social risk" is not difficult for social workers; some high social risk situations include: the very old who are unattached and live alone; elderly couples when severe illness is suffered by one partner; the single parent with children under 16 years of age; patients with diagnoses—such as renal disease or hemophilia—which could imply severe social and physical limitations. These are obviously characteristics which can be found among outpatients as well as inpatients. Discovering patients with social problems which affect their ability to benefit from medical care conforms to the basic philosophy of social work in a health setting. In this context social work is responsible for its own case-finding, and needs to assure access to service. Thus social workers, using their experience, combined with high risk variables, the physician's prediction, and the predicted length-of-stay inventory used by the medical institution, should be able to uncover patients with social problems. Services should become available to people at any of the potential stress points accompanying illness and affecting them and/or family members. In the case of hospitalized patients, this may mean passing over most short-stay patients, except those referred, or those maternal and neonatal situations in which high social risks are evident regardless of hospital stay. Social services in specialized hospitals, averaging short stays, but dealing with tertiary care, such as sensory disorders, must find those at risk when admission is being planned, but no later than "at admission." Patients expected to leave the hospital in less than ten days may have to be perceived as undergoing a more or less transitory experience; if social problems exist, such patients may need to seek services elsewhere, and for them, an information and referral service may be the primary social service. In general acute and long-stay institutions, social work will concentrate on the longer stay patients, probably those with chronic diseases, but will begin its interventions early.

When social work undertakes pre-admission or at-admission work-ups in special and high social risk situations, the social-psychological information can be made available to physicians early, permitting a more comprehensive approach to diagnosis and to treatment. Pre-admission or at-admission screening can also strongly affect the hospitalization experience for the individual and the quality of the discharge planning, an interprofessional responsibility which must include the patient and/or his family as participants in the process. If social work starts by planning for return home no later than or even before admission, a climate can be created that signifies hospitalization in its transitory therapeutic sense, while readying the kin and home for homecoming. Although specific post-hospital care may not be known early in the caring process, the intent for discharge would have been projected. The acute hospital experience would be regarded as transitory but purposeful, which it is for the majority of hospitalized patients, albeit eventful. This method also involves the family members early in commitment to the patient's

care. Regular visiting at the hospital is one component; investment in the discharge plan is another. Experiments of this kind
have demonstrated that the outcomes of social work services
have critically affected the length of stay, shortening it by one
day or more. These outcomes certainly affected the quality of the
hospitalization and of the discharge plan, by involving the patient and his family in their own behalf. These experiments also
prove that sound and comprehensive discharge planning requires skilled social work intervention.

New Skills, Programs, and Collaboration

Early intervention resulting from early case-finding requires that
social work be critically involved in what it means to become and
to be a patient. New skills and roles little activated in the past,
because of the profession's dependence on the referral system,
are required, new ways to begin with prospective clients, no
longer depending on the referrer's request for service. The social
worker must develop skills in initiating contact with the patient
and his family members concerning situational and personal social needs. The worker's question on beginning with a client is:
"How do I start without knowing a presenting problem?" The
start affects not only what the worker learns but also the client's
motivation to cooperate on the identified social problem. Early
intervention demands understanding of the effect of specific diseases and disorders on both physical and social functioning, as
well as general knowledge of the illness and the ability to in-
dividualize to the given patient and his situation. Social workers
are aware that illness patterns change, and that social and physical functioning change, too. Early intervention means early social diagnosis and social assessment. When it is possible to special-
ize among the more common disorders treated in the institution,
particularly the chronic diseases, social workers show closer collaboration with other health care professionals serving the same
patients a key factor in achieving a more effective comprehen
sive approach to patients' and families' social and medical needs.
Therefore, where concentration in specific disorders with a given
number of health care professionals (doctors and nurses, in particular), takes place, greater social work contribution to the comprehensiveness of the diagnosis and the treatment, as well as to

convalescence and rehabilitation, can be expected.

Social work needs to go on record, to take a risk, in projecting social assessments in relation to the medical assessment; this means working more quickly from the current situation and observed behaviors of the patient and his family, with little time for extensive social history taking. Having usually been limited to post-hospital planning, social workers in medical care services have done little in contributing to diagnostic formulations. Early entry into patient-family situations enables social workers to cooperate very differently with physicians from the outset, integrating the social with the medical for joint assessment and joint therapeutic and convalescent planning.

With changing societal patterns in bed utilization, and as social workers concentrate more on long-stay patients early in their hospitalizations, the work will increasingly be with the very sick and very disabled, the "legitimated" longer stays. Undoubtedly the result will be heavier social service case loads because more patients and families with social problems will be uncovered. At the same time, skillful intervention in dealing with high social-psychological risks, compounded by severity of illness or by exacerbation of chronic disease, will be required. This combination means that manpower will have to be used differentially. Counseling and supportive care in relation to social and physical functioning, and environmental services in seeking out needed social resources such as extended care facilities, at-home services, and appliances will call for different staffing patterns. Because of the anticipated high demands, it is expected that community resources will be even less available than at present. Counseling patients and families to utilize their own resources, internal and external, will be more essential than ever.

In all probability social work will offer its services in the form of contracts or goals mutually agreed upon by the client and the social worker. Now practice generally evolves from the worker's or the referrer's perception of problem. Social workers have hitherto tended to work in a more open-ended, fluid approach, concentrating essentially on relationship, on the assumption that relationship therapy will cause the patient to work on the problem or to change his behavior as a result of the transference. Experience to date reveals less resolution of problems through relationship as the major factor, and a large number of incom-

plete or dropout situations that may be a result of this expectation. Contracts, where the practice exists, have already demonstrated that the *length* of social work services *is* affected, that
client and worker satisfaction *is* readily evidenced, and that a
greater positive resolution of agreed-upon problems, worked on
together *is* achieved. The patient and family are realistically
ready to undertake social problem-oriented contracts. People
clearly comprehend what it means to have problems and to seek
help for them; social workers need to define what is most critical
with clients, not attempt to deal with all the problems facing
them. Patients do want an active part in problem solving; where
this does not occur, dropouts or failure tend to follow; if clients
take an active part, the outcome or satisfaction with services
tends to improve. Contract-making and interprofessional collaboration call for great skill, knowledge of personality, of the psy-
chodynamics of behavior, of family interaction, of communication theory, and of the sociocultural factors in the client system
and the health care system. When social workers work with contracts, they must be concerned with "what happened," the "outcome," "were the mutually-agreed-upon goals achieved." If the
goals were not achieved, then the reason must be examined, not
assumed to be a failure within the client only.

In short-stay hospitals, social workers have limited opportunity to extend hospitalization while seeking resources for post-
hospital care. Already there are few, if any, accepted social reasons for extending a hospital stay, unless support is achieved by
social action. Where gaps in service fail to meet the needs of
individuals and families, organized social workers, other health
care personnel, and consumers must join together to lobby and
negotiate for more and improved services for people in their own
homes.

While social work has begun to face an increased demand for
its services on behalf of hospitalized patients, an even greater
need will be evident among ambulatory patients, whether pre-
admission, post hospital, or those whose illness does not require
hospitalization. Rather than being limited to abortive or crisis-
planned after-care, with comparatively little post-hospital continuity of its services, work will be with patients and families whose
preexistent social needs impede sound convalescence, rehabilitation, and recovery. A major emphasis for social work services in

the future will be either in institutional outpatient programs, or in free-standing social work service programs linked to medical care and attached in some way to the institution. The work will concentrate on implementing comprehensive care, coordinating services, developing motivation in clients to use these, and introducing patient- and family-oriented social health educational programs. New funding and/or fees for the services of social therapy clinics will have to be found. The demand for such social treatment programs related to illness, and requiring some minimal medical intervention, will have to be demonstrated by studies or by pilot programs. Social work services will be income-producing to the hospital, either directly or via third-party or fee-for-service reimbursement; some already are. Social work will also assume responsibility for affecting bed occupancy rates, by recruiting patients in need of inpatient care from given community programs such as specialized child screening efforts.

There are many social situations in relation to illnesses and diseases in which education of patients and their families should be the first approach or even the answer to service need. Education in self-care is certainly clearly needed by patients such as diabetics, coronaries, hemophiliacs, and the obese. While some group programs exist, has the profession considered open-ended educational groups for individuals with specific diseases, as continuing after-care services? Social work has all the skills needed: group techniques, motivational development, empathy, knowledge of the process of human interrelationships, and of the effect of culture on behavior. No physician nor other health care professional possesses this combination of skills.

Documenting Social Work Services
for the Record

The annotation of social work services in the medical chart is mandated by federal regulations and by many standard-setting bodies which serve to accredit medical institutions and to safeguard quality; in addition, third-party reimbursement agencies demand the documentation of services for which payment is claimed. Standards promulgated by the National Association of Social Workers and by the Society for Hospital Social Work Directors have made documentation a standard of service.

Apart from the requirement as a standard for social work practice in a medical setting, a range of benefits are gained from the social work services entry in a medical chart. The medical record, the primary tool of all the health care professionals serving a patient, also serves as a communication medium, annotating diagnostic formulations, therapeutic maintenance, and the health care direction and recommendations for a patient. The chart's social work entry is visible to others, and thus has the potential for use in professional deliberations of care. Quality social work annotations can contribute to diagnostic considerations, affect the therapeutic direction, unquestionably introduce comprehensiveness into the caring and services, and can enhance the collaborative relationships among health care professionals. The written chart entry is openly recognized as valuable by other disciplines, who use the content and follow-up with verbal interaction on behalf of the patient as part of interprofessional planning for his or her care.

Even though social workers remain uncertain, the author believes chart notation can reflect "good" practice. There is every indication that a professional social work staff can meet the mandate placed on it and do so professionally. Chart notating is easy for new workers to incorporate into practice, through early orientation as a department standard. The adjustment has been more difficult for the more experienced, who have for a long time been conducting their practice in their own style. While a natural peer protectiveness tends to appear at introduction of the standard, professional expectations tend to prevail. Those who cannot tolerate structural standards may drop out. Use of peer group planning and reenforcement for social work chart entries gives the process its professional base and increases the opportunity to improve the means of meeting the purposes in the most efficient, qualitative ways.

Almost all staff members comment that the chart notation sharpens thinking, adds clarity, and gives structure to practice, that having order and purposiveness in the counseling process through contracted agreements and assessed outcomes is meaningful and assists in improvement of practice by forcing examination of the problem and its resolution in professional terms.

The written entry is a traditional educational tool; social work notes in the medical chart have even greater educational potential, since they must be a logical component of the whole. In time, the notations may, with special considerations and with staff training, have research potential. In any event, they are utilized for peer review, for support of the social work services audit, and can be used for an interprofessional audit when refined for that purpose.

Information Systems, Auditing and Peer Review, and Continuing Education

Any system involved in providing services to the public requires the means to secure information and retrieval of meaningful data concerning delivery of those services. The information sought should be specific to the institution and its departments, but must also safeguard the availability of information which is regionally or nationally significant.

Some have called for uniform approaches to data collection, noting that the information would be for the common good. Uniformity has been all but impossible to secure, and the author questions whether there need be the same system for all. It is certainly possible to report data uniformly for the general needs of all institutions and professions, leaving each to secure, in addition, what it needs for its own purposes. Where standards for specific practices may have more uniformity, these may need to be perceived within principles general enough to allow for regional retrieval but allowing for individual, yet acceptable, differences. The overall reviewing bodies now call for the implementation of quality assurance programs, in principle, leaving the monitoring to local efforts, but subjecting the processes to review. Since all medical institutions in a given area contribute to the combined services rendered the local population, they will be expected to view the information for its quality, for its capacity to meet needs, and for the gaps indicated in sound and comprehensive care.

To develop quality assurance programs, data collection must avoid accumulating vast amounts of unusable information. What is secured should be meaningful and significant to the practitioner, in the single and collective sense, to assure an effective response. Successful audit and peer review must involve the practitioner in the subject (or services) under review. Communication between professional practitioners and their peer reviewers is therefore essential. The profession itself must have evolved the standards and criteria utilized in review and have contributed to the reviewing modalities. Audits can be effective if they employ study methods which touch on items and components meaningful to delivery of service, which reflect their importance in affecting the patient and his family's welfare, and which demonstrate areas for needed improvement. The peer review should be based on criteria acceptable to the professional group, supported by clinical research methods, and its findings communicated via direct interaction between the reviewers and the practitioners under review. The peer review is specific to the performance of professionals on behalf of their clients, the audit concerns issues of delivery of care in given locales, for disease-specifics, for special procedures or defined subjects for assessment. Both processes are essential for monitoring of care and both are rooted in information, data, and evaluation. The basic expectations from each are the improvement of services by correcting the problems uncovered and support of the need for changing practices by the continuous education of the practitioners.

Gathering information need not be left exclusively either to peers or other agents, but can be done by the professional himself. It is but one step from a single case assessment to analysis of clusters of situations carried by the individual social worker. Self-evaluation and accountability should be in the basic armamentarium of each practitioner. For social work in hospitals, each worker has within his or her practice a range of patient/family situations which have reached him or her within a given context, seeking help with given social problems which have significance for the disease or illness. To ask, "Who is my client?" "What is the problem?" "What is the illness?" "What is being sought?" "What was offered?" "By whom?" "What happened as a result?" is as pertinent to the multiple client systems as to the single case. To be curious about one's practice and to use one's own direct services to seek out answers contribute to self-assessment. Simple questions and their answers become applied studies, professionally attuned, leading to self-directedness and self-evaluation, the sine qua non of a mature professional.

Peer review and audits should be developed by each profession for its own professional monitoring. Peer review will always be the province of the given profession to screen its own practitioners. However, audits in health care settings may well (and probably should) assume a multi-professional dimension. Although difficulties still exist in the way physicians view non-medical health care practitioners in caring for patients, cooperation among fields of endeavor in comprehensive care has currency. It is now generally accepted that the biological-medical fields alone cannot provide what is needed to care for the sick and to maintain the healthy. Interdependence of the social and biomedical systems makes necessary the development of multi-professional audits. These are possible even though their beginnings have reflected the difficulties of the participating professions in having others look over their practice shoulders. As peer review has been an educational process for the reviewers, so has the multi-professional audit advanced the knowledge of others' practices and even viewing one's own.

Each quality assurance program carries the expectation that action will be taken to correct uncovered deficits in care. Such action may be to secure administrative or departmental change in the way the particular service is rendered. In any event, implementation requires a change in the behaviors of the administrative and/or practice professional. This change can be secured if the feedback loop from reviewer to practitioner is interactional, with direct and personal communication. Direct interaction is imperative for the significance of the practice and to learn the most desirable change from the practitioners themselves. Without the practitioners' involvement in the planned change, the future of the improvement is doubtful. Their involvement also safeguards the motivation for continuous education to achieve new behaviors and practices, and to participate in the regular reassessment of delivery of services.

Assessing quality of care in the education of the student professional is useful for teaching the use of criteria and standards of care, assessment as a process and as self-review, and for developing a future orientation to ongoing self-evaluation and service review. Evidence already shows that the professional's investment in review does affect his practice, making it more focused, more self-evaluative, clearer about role and function, and increasingly collaborative.

The PSRO legislation calls for a "qualified" professional who will remain continually qualified, informed on new knowledge in delivery of services. If individual review and audits are effective, then the feedback is expected to make professionals respond to continuing study. Agencies, social work schools, and professional associations will need to provide ongoing periodic educational opportunities for practitioners, based on demonstrated practice needs. Since making educational resources available does not assure a professional's use of them, incentives must be introduced. Continuing education will be mandatory for all service professions, with the primary incentive, relicensing or recertification. Several state medical and nurses' associations have already projected the linkage between continuing education or re-examinations for relicensing on a periodic basis.

Fee-for-Service, Vendor Status, and the Consumer

Reimbursement for delivery of social work services in health care is now with us: the cost of care is built into general accounting statements, either as a specific budgeted social work program or as a wage-cost component of another service in the hospital where social work exists. Social work services have been provided for in legislative programs such as Medicare and Medicaid. The problem for the profession is that the extent of services provided in hospitals is left largely to administrative, medical, or lay board determination; none of these bodies is adequately informed of the importance of the services to patients. Neither social workers nor their clients have been sufficiently vocal in translating social work's contribution to comprehensiveness of care; however, surveys and studies have recently demonstrated the value, and social workers and their clients have used these data to speak for the programs. The National Association of Social Workers has addressed the professional issues by its programs, in support of defining levels of competency, of state licensing and certification, of vendorship status and third party coverage, and by lobbying to include social work services in all appropriate legislative projections.

As social services become a basic component of comprehensive health care and are paid for, through salaried positions in programs or as fee-for-service in health care settings or private practice, consumers will expect a "say" about the services given

—one concerned with what is given, by whom, within certain expected professional standards. Professional accountability will be to the client, the consumer of social services. In the future, the consumer and the provider will review, assess, and plan together. The National Health Planning and Resources Development Act, P.L. 93-641 has projected the Health Systems Agency (HSA) as the means for such planning. HSAs, regional and local, in their present or a revised format, will probably furnish a key linkage to provider accountability, institutional and professional. In determining health care resources for a community or a region, the HSA will undoubtedly seek some relationship to PSRO, and other agencies, in order to judge the quality and cost-effectiveness of services delivered.

The consumer's voice has begun to be heard. Growing criticism of medical care has resulted in legislation and regulation. In this sense, a systematic, respected consumer assessment of health care and its social work component is expected to contribute to quality. Consumers emphasize improved care and increased satisfaction with care, both institutional and by the professional provider. Consumers still lack information about comprehensive care, quality, competency, prices, services, drugs, specialties, and more; they have not been sufficiently involved in decision making about their own medical care, let alone the general situation. This is true for social work services as well. Consumers are caught up in the peculiarities of third-party payment systems, which are still provider-oriented and dominated. Consumers now have no relationship to the monitoring of licensure, accreditation, or professional discipline. For consumers to deal with the social health care system will require demystification of delivery of care, of medical and social illness and their treatment, and of the roles, responsibilities, and costs of the many different health care professionals. The proliferation of self-help groups that deal with social health maintenance is evidence that people are seeking more than they get from the medical and social service systems of care. It is expected that consumer advocacy or ombudsmanship in relation to social health care will appear under some governmental auspice, both nationally and locally, as one approach to consumer involvement. HSAs are already functioning. A more critical voice on third-party payers' boards should be anticipated. The consumer's entry into the social health arena will lead to more searching knowledge about professional providers, what they have to offer, how well they perform, and at what cost.

Regionalization and Its Implications
for Social Work

The concept of regionalization means different things to different people and institutions. Some suggest that regionalization is an abrogation of autonomy of practice, while others believe it is the only means of resolving the problems of duplication, overutilization, fragmentation, and episodic care. The issue of autonomy is an illusion in that there are no medical institutions (and there should be no service professions) without regulatory overseers. Furthermore, the government, under the pressure of professional and provider associations, has promulgated voluntary surveillance of quality assurance, allowing the hospitals and the health care professions to monitor themselves.

Regionalization is a programmatic approach to health care, drawing on the service network of an area and its population. Regionalization means more than providers' sharing of purchasing programs, billing, and equipment; it should include the definition of resources, their relevance and appropriateness to the entire population, not only the currently sick, but those served and to-be-served, and to their social health needs for health maintenance. Both providers and consumers will be needed to bring joint deliberation to regional planning.

If social health care is approached at the regional level, a number of new organizational designs must be considered. In addition to those suggested for consumers finding their relationship to providers, as in HSAs and forums for their own special interests, providers will need and want to consider regional, as well as individual, concerns. Social workers in health care, as providers, will seek to join together as regional providers to deal with common issues, and as individual professionals to deal with overall professional issues.

As a first step, leaders of social work programs within a region should join together to identify the information and data needed. While the data to be sought will be uniform in definition and in reporting to serve the common purpose, it need not jeopardize autonomy in data collection for individual institutions. A regional data base means that each system and subsystem, in addition to answering its individual requirements, also contributes to regional needs so that overall planning and programming can take place. A uniform, regionalized approach does not mean that every hospital nor every service is assessed in the same terms; comparability will have to be defined. Teaching hospitals and those with specialized programs and staffing are clearly not comparable to general community hospitals.

Social work must examine not only overall departmental services provided, but also the specialized areas. One cannot assume that what is required in pediatrics is also required in adult surgery, nor that each demands the same caliber or amount of social services. When these questions are reviewed for the region, then population needs, and available and missing resources can also be considered.

Some advantages of regional social work deliberations are:

1. Common denominators are available; standardization can be achieved; flexibility in the use of different programs and practices is possible.
2. Systematic shared study methods become more readily possible:
   a. To determine social needs of patient populations
   b. To determine the services required to meet these needs
   c. To assess the services rendered
   d. To determine sound program priorities in service
3. The data and information gathered contribute to the development of professionally accepted norms, criteria, and standards for practice.
4. Working in groups, on both administrative and practice levels, when not limited to one setting, can be invigorating and bring more comprehensive interpretations to others, such as hospital administrators, boards, consumer groups, third-party payers, and the profession.
5. A regional system should help to determine where demand exists at given points in time, and thus help with aspects of staff assignment and program planning.

6. Direct service units and their costs can be jointly determined, the differences understood, and programs interpreted as a regional approach to delivery of services.

7. Cost assignments can be considered differentially, by identifying the counseling and motivating programs and the support services, such as at-home health aides, homemakers, meals-on-wheels, nursing home placements, family planning, substance abuse, and others.

8. Studies performed in one setting can be replicated in others, while experimental studies can be performed in multiple settings.

9. Continuous educational needs can be uncovered and provision to meet them addressed at the regional level.

10. Orientation and special training programs can be jointly designed and provided, under common auspices.

11. A forum can be established for social workers in the region and can, in turn, create a common voice for the profession, dealing with professional concerns as well as with social action on behalf of consumers' needs.

The professional organizations, such as the metropolitan or regional chapters of the National Association of Social Workers, the Society for Hospital Social Work Directors, the Federation of Clinical Social Workers, the regional schools of social work, and others could lend their members or faculty to such regional forums, thereby contributing to and benefitting by the interaction. Under these joint auspices, continuing educational opportunities could be provided. The orientation and training of social workers in dealing with the regionalization of social work services could be undertaken under a regional council for social work services.

Quality assurance programs to date have been cost-effective. The length of stay in hospitals has been reduced, some excesses, such as prescribed drug use, and, more recently, unnecessary surgical procedures, have been removed or cut back. The quality of care has begun to improve. Some programs offering more comprehensiveness have been introduced. Consumers are better informed and have had more basic health education. Records have undoubtedly improved as a result of professional review.

There are, however, more regulation, increased costs of care, more paper work, more defensive medicine, more directives, and uncertainty that there will be much more improvement or more equity in distribution or better access to services. However, the journey into quality assurance has only begun. The profession has much to do; institutions will be reshaped, and the consumer will have his say in their reshaping.

Exhibits 1 through 20

EXHIBIT 1

<u>HSR Screening Form</u>

Category I.   Automatic Social Work Assistant Review- high social risk
identified as:

_____   1. Over 70 years, living alone, with eye surgery projected

_____   2. Institutional transfers into the hospital

Category II. Social Worker Review- High Social Risk identified as:

_____   1. 80 year old and over

_____   2. 70 year old and over, living alone

_____   3. Emergency admission

(except appendicitis, hernias, pneumonias)

_____   4. Severity of illness- life threatening

(i.e. metastatic or terminal CA and blood dyscrasias,
all admissions to ND, CICU, Ames, CT, RT)

_____   5. Severity of illness- physical dysfunctioning

(i.e. organic and/or mental brain syndrome, encephalo-
pathies; syrengo-myelia; CVA and stroke, aphasia, patho-
logical fractures; carcinoma of the colon, rectum,
pancreas, brain or masses leading to "ostomies;" any
limb surgery leading to amputation; (due to diabetes,
gangrene, circulatory diseases); carcinoma of the
throat, vocal chord, larynx, tongue, airway obstructions
leading to "ectomies;" renal diseases leading to dialysis
and/or transplant; multiple fractures; eye disorders i.e.
glaucoma, retinal detachment, conditions which are
sight threatening.)

_____   6. Chronic Diseases

(i.e. lupus, Hodgkins, myasthenia gravis, ulcerative colitis,
multiple sclerosis, cerebral palsy, hemophilia, sickle
cell, muscular dystrophy, rheumatoid arthritis, liver
diseases.)

EXHIBIT 2

Department of Social Services

STAFF ACTIVITIES
(Not Direct Services)

Month/Year _____

Staff Member _____

Date	IDENTIFICATION OF ACTIVITY (Name of person, committee, organization, community group, etc.)	Type of and Time Spent* on Activity									Specify Objective
		1	2(a) Education	2(b)	2(c)	3	4	5	6	7	
		Staff Development	Social Work Students	Medical Students	Other Health Care Professions	Policy, Program and Procedural Planning	Rounds, Patient Care Discussion Groups	Peer Review/Audits	Research	Other	

*Time should be in minutes to the nearest 15, 30, 45 or 60 minutes.

SSD #M-12

171

EXHIBIT 3

THE MOUNT SINAI HOSPITAL, NEW YORK   SOCIAL SERVICE DEPARTMENT

7 MONTH 8	9 DAY 10	YEAR	11	UNIT NO.	16	17	SERIAL NO.	22		23	WORKER NO.	27

28	PATIENT LAST NAME	40	41	PATIENT FIRST NAME	49	WORKER NAME

50 PATIENT CODE (CIRCLE ONE)	REGISTERED WITH OTHER WORKER	REGISTRATION FORM
3 –IN PATIENT 4 –OUT PATIENT		

SERVICES: ENTER CODE ONCE FOR EACH TIME A SERVICE IS PERFORMED. EXAMPLE: | 36 | 46 | 57 | 60 | 48 | 36 | 57 |

CODES FOR SERVICES

DIRECT SERVICES		SUPPORTIVE SERVICES		
INSIDE	OUTSIDE	INSIDE	TELEPHONE	OUTSIDE
36 PATIENT 41			PT/CORE GRP →54	52 COMM HEW
37 CORE GROUP MBR. 42		46 DOCTOR 55		53 OTHER
38 JT-PT/CORE GRP 43		48 OTHER MSH 56		
39 GROUP A 44		49 3 DISC JT		**MISCELLANEOUS**
40 GROUP B 45		50 COMM HEW 57		59 REPORT, FORMS
47 JT-PT/CORE & PROF 61		51 OTHER 58		60 CORRESPONDENCE

USES FOR REGISTRATION FORM (CHECK APPROPRIATE BOX)

R 75		REGISTER ONLY
C 75		REGISTER & CLOSE CASE — EVALUATION (76 77) SERVICE (78 79)
T 75		REGISTER AND TRANSFER CASE TO: WORKER NAME ___ WORKER NUMBER (76 77 78 79 80)

51		OPENING CODE 1 NEW 2 REOPENED	BIRTH DATE	SOCIAL SECURITY NO.
52–55		LAST CLOSED month/year	ADDRESS (No. & Street)	
56		RESIDENCE CODE		
57		SEX 1 - M 2 - F 3 - NK	BOROUGH OR CITY/STATE	ZIP NO.
58–59		AGE IN YEARS	CARE OF	
60		MARITAL STAT 1-S 2-M 3-W 4-D 5-Sep 6-Com L 7-UM 8-NK	FLOOR OR APT. NO.	SIZE OF APT.
61		RELIGION 1-J 2-C 3-P 4-Oth 5-NK	TELEPHONE NO.	RENT
62		ETHNIC GRP 1-W 2-N 3-PR 4-Oth 5-NK		
63		EMP STAT 1-Full/t 2-Part/t 3-Ret 4-Unempl 5-Not A 6-NK	* COUNTRY OF BIRTH	MOTHER'S MAIDEN NAME
64		OCCUPATION	* EMPLOYER'S NAME	
65–66		MED. DIAG.	* EMPLOYER'S ADDRESS	
67–68		SERVICE		
69–70		LOCATION 1-PRIV 2-SP 3-SPD, 4-CL 5-AC 6-ER 7-HC 8-SAT 9-SCP 10-EC 11-OTHR 12-NK	* EMPLOYER'S TEL. NO.	
71–72		REFERRAL 1-Dr 2-N 3-Self 4-Fam 5-Adm 6-WSc 7-100% 8-OA 9-Oth 10-NK	NAME OF SCHOOL	
74		NUMBER OF HOUSEHOLD MEMBERS	CURRENT ADMISSION DATE	DISCHARGE DATE

RELATIONSHIP TO PATIENT	DATE OF BIRTH	COUNTRY OF BIRTH	UNIT NO.	EMPLOYED YES	NO

LIST NAMES

INTERESTED PERSONS – PHYSICIANS – AGENCIES	IDENTIFY	ADDRESS	TELEPHONE NO.

MEDICARE NUMBER	MA OFFICE	MEDICAID NUMBER	SUFFIX	DSS NUMBER AND CENTER

* IF PATIENT IS UNDER 16, GIVE THIS INFORMATION WITH REGARD TO PARENT.

FORM M-18 10M 6-77 CAMELOT

SSD REGISTRATION FORM

EXHIBIT 4

SOCIAL SERVICE DAILY TRANSACTIONS

07

MONTH DAY YEAR
7 8 9 10

WORKER NAME

4 4
23 24

WORKER NUMBER
31 32 33 34 35

A
36

| PATIENT NAME | | UNIT NO. | SERIAL NUMBER | CHARGE AMOUNT | PATIENT CODE 3—IN 4—OUT | REG. WITH OTHER WORKER | | CODES FOR SERVICES | | | |
| LAST NAME | FIRST NAME | 11—16 | 17—22 | 25—30 | 27 | 38 | | | | | |

CODES FOR SERVICES

| DIRECT SERVICES | | SUPPORTIVE SERVICES | | | |
| INSIDE | OUTSIDE | INSIDE | TELEPHONE OUTSIDE | | |

36 PATIENT	41	PT CORE GRP→ 54	57 COMM HEW
37 CORE GROUP HBR	42 46	DOCTOR 55	53 OTHER
38 JT.PT CORE GRP	43 48	OTHER HEW	56
			MISCELLANEOUS
39 GROUP A	44 49	3 DIST JT	
40 GROUP B	45 50	COMM HEW 57	59 REPORT, FORMS
4 JT.PT CORE & PROF 81	51	OTHER 58	60 CORRESPONDENCE

FOR SERVICES ENTER CODE NUMBER ONCE FOR EACH TIME A SERVICE
IS PERFORMED, EXAMPLE:

| 36 | 46 | 57 | 60 | 48 | 36 | 57 |
39—80

FORM M-188 12—78 ABG

173

EXHIBIT 5

FORM M-1

10M 12/77 Camelot

THE MOUNT SINAI HOSPITAL
SOCIAL SERVICES DEPARTMENT

CHANGE OF STATUS/CLOSING

7	MONTH	8	9	DAY	10	YEAR	11	UNIT NO.	16	PATIENT'S NAME LAST		FIRST

T R A N S	17	\	BOX	WORKER TRANSFERRED TO			WORKER TRANSFERRED FROM		
			18	NUMBER	22	NAME	NUMBER		NAME

C L O S E D	23	\	BOX	CLOSING EVALUATION	24 CDE 25	CLOSING SERVICE	26 CDE 27

PATIENT IDENTIFICATION AND PROFILE CORRECTIONS

28	\	BOX	29	LAST NAME	41	42	FIRST NAME	50	51	WORKER NO.	55

56 PATIENT CODE

CIRCLE CORRECTION   1 - PREADMISSION IN   3 - INPATIENT   4 - OUTPATIENT   5 - POST HOSPITAL
2 - PREADMISSION OUT

COL.	NEW CODE		COL.	NEW CODE	
57		OPENING CODE 1 - NEW 2 - REOPENED	69		EMPLOYMENT STATUS 1 - FULL/T 2 - PART/T 3 - RET 4 - UNEMP 5 - NOT-A 6 - NK
58 to 61		MONTH & YEAR LAST CLOSED	70		OCCUPATION
62		RESIDENCE CODE	71 to 72		MEDICAL DIAGNOSIS
		ADDRESS STREET ADDRESS BOROUGH OR CITY/STATE ZIP NO.	73 to 74		SERVICE
63		SEX 1 - M 2 - F 3 - NK	75 to 78		LOCATION 1 - PRIV 2 - SP 3 - SPD 4 - CL 5 - AC 6 - ER 7 - HC 8 - SAT 9 - SCP 10 - EC 11 - OTHR 12 - NK
64 to 65		AGE IN YEARS			
66		MARITAL STATUS 1 - S 2 - M 3 - W 4 - D 5 - SEP 6 - COM L 7 - UM 8 - NK	77 to 78		REFERRAL 1 - DR 2 - N 3 - SELF 4 - FAM 5 - ADM 6 - WSC 7 - 100% 8 - OA 9 - OTH 10 - NK
67		RELIGION 1 - J 2 - C 3 - P 4 - OTH 5 - NK	79		PRE–ADMISSION (PSYCHIATRY ONLY) 1 - IND 2 - OUTP 3 - NA 4 - NK
68		ETHNIC GRP 1 - W 2 - N 3 - PR 4 - OTH 5 - NK	80		NUMBER OF HOUSEHOLD MEMBERS

PREPARED BY_____   _____   _____
WORKER'S NAME   WORKER'S NUMBER   DATE

DATA PROCESSING COPY

174

EXHIBIT 6

NO. WORK DAYS _____   TOTAL SHEET

MONTH ENDING   UNIT

	WORKERS OR SUPERVISORS									TOTAL
The Mount Sinai Hospital SSD REPORT OF CASELOAD ACTIVITY M 7B										
CARRIED FORWARD										
OPENED THIS MONTH — New										
OPENED THIS MONTH — Reopened										
OPENED THIS MONTH — TOTAL OPENED										
TRANSFERS TO										
TOTAL OPEN										
TRANSFERS FROM										
CLOSED THIS MONTH										
CARRIED FORWARD										
Active this Month										
Inactive this Month										
INSIDE — Patient 36										
INSIDE — Core Grp. Member 37										
INSIDE — Jt/Pt Core Grp 38										
INSIDE — Group A 39										
INSIDE — Group B 40										
OUTSIDE — Patient 41										
OUTSIDE — Core Grp Member 42										
OUTSIDE — Jt/Pt Core Grp 43										
OUTSIDE — Group A 44										
OUTSIDE — Group B 45										
OUTSIDE — Jt/Pt Core Prof 47 61										
TOTAL DIRECT SERVICES										
INSIDE — Doctor 46										
INSIDE — Other MSH 48										
INSIDE — 3 Disc Joint 49										
INSIDE — Comm. HEW Agencies 50										
INSIDE — Other 51										
OUTSIDE — Comm. HEW Agencies 52										
OUTSIDE — Other 53										
TELE PHONES — Pt/Core Group 54										
TELE PHONES — Doctor 55										
TELE PHONES — Other MSH 56										
TELE PHONES — Comm. HEW Agencies 57										
TELE PHONES — Other 58										
REPORTS & FORMS 59										
CORRESPONDENCE 60										
TOTAL SUPPORTIVE SERVICES										
COURTESY SERVICES — INTERVIEWS										
COURTESY SERVICES — TELEPHONE										
COURTESY SERVICES — CORRESPONDENCE										

DIRECT SERVICES (spanning INSIDE, OUTSIDE rows)

SUPPORTIVE SERVICES (spanning TELE PHONES and related rows)

EXHIBIT 7

DRAFT PROCEDURE

SUBJECT: REPORTING FOR THE SYSTEM FOR HOSPITAL UNIFORM REPORTING (SHUR)

Index Under	File #	Date
Operational Functions, Policies and Procedures	Section 2 Item 2-9	Issued 12/78

Auspice

This data reporting is required under the Federal Medicare and Medicaid Anti-fraud Act.

Who Will Report

California and N.Y. State have been selected as pilots. Thus, reporting by all hospitals in these states is mandated. Reporting is done by all Hospital Departments.

The Reporting System

Mount Sinai Social Work Services Department's prior work has formed the base for the reporting system for social work. The problem classification part of the system was tested in New England (4,000 cases). It will be further tested nationally as a part of a study employing several methods. This study is jointly sponsored by the Society for Hospital Social Work Directors and the NASW, funded by voluntary contributions from hospitals via Social Work Departments requests. Dr. Claudia Coulton of Case Western Reserve heads the national study.

Although revisions of the reporting system will undeniably be developed, for the next 2 years the system described below must be used by N.Y. State and California.

When

Starts January 1, 1979.

MANUAL OF POLICIES AND PROCEDURES
SOCIAL SERVICE DEPARTMENT

EXHIBIT 7 (continued)

SUBJECT: REPORTING FOR THE SYSTEM FOR HOSPITAL UNIFORM REPORTING (SHUR)

Index Under	File #	Date
Operational Functions, Policies and Procedures	Section 2 Item 2-9	Issued 12/78

What is Counted

This system is an attempt to count the cost of providing social work services to patients. Activities are counted in such a way as to reflect indirect as well as direct services to patients.

Cases are not the unit counted. Quality is not costed out. Activities, weighted by a relative value system based on time, are the measure of count.

Activities Counted

Three types of activities are counted:

    I. Screeening

   II. Assessment

  III. Problem Focused Intervention

Fixed relative values are assigned to each of the three activities, according to a level of complexity ratio. Each unit equals 10 minutes.

     (a) All Screenings have a fixed level of complexity - relative value of 2 units (20 minutes)

     (b) All Assessments have a fixed R.V.U. of 6 (60 minutes)

     (c) Problem-Focused Services are fixed by a formula combining number of problems with number of visits for out-patients and length of hospital stay for in-patients

     (d) Ambulatory care groups - 8 units for each group meeting.

The fixed value is an average which "washes out" differences. For example some screenings take two minutes, some forty. The 20 minutes fixed value is a wash out average. This also applies to assessment which is fixed for 60 minutes, though some take more time, some less.

MANUAL OF POLICIES AND PROCEDURES
SOCIAL SERVICE DEPARTMENT

EXHIBIT 7 (continued)

SUBJECT: REPORTING FOR THE SYSTEM FOR HOSPITAL UNIFORM REPORTING (SHUR)

(page 3 of 6 pages)

Index Under	File #	Date
Operational Functions, Policies and Procedures	Section 2 Item 2-9	Issued 12/78

How Data Will be Collected (Data Source)

I.   In Patient

   A.   In Patient Screenings

      1.   The Following will be Reported and Credited as Screenings

         a.   Adult Medical Surgical In Patient

            High Risk Screening Criteria will be used.

         b.   Psychiatry In Patient

            Every admission is screened by a social worker.

         c.   Pediatrics In Patient

            Neo Natal Admissions are screened by a social worker. High Risk criteria will be used for other Pediatrics In-Patients.

         d.   Obstetrics

            See Out-Patient Section of this procedure. As yet there is no system developed for counting in-patient screenings in Obstetrics.

   B.   In Patient Assessments

      Each opened case will be credited for an assessment.

   C.   In Patient Problem Focused Intervention

      Each opened case will be counted and R.V.U. assigned according to length of hospital stay and number of problems. The staff member, at the time of patient's discharge from the hospital, will fill in the problem classification form specifying -

MANUAL OF POLICIES AND PROCEDURES
SOCIAL SERVICE DEPARTMENT

EXHIBIT 7 (continued)

SUBJECT: REPORTING FOR THE SYSTEM FOR HOSPITAL UNIFORM REPORTING (SHUR)

(page 4 of 6 pages)

Index Under	File #	Date
Operating Functions, Policies and Procedures	Section 2 Item 2-9	Issued 12/78

1. The date of admission

2. Date of discharge

3. Problems dealt with

4. Outcome of problems

5. Total number of problems dealt with. The worker will transmit the completed problem sheets with the regular daily statistical forms.

Note:

    If social work intervention continues after discharge from the hospital, another problem classification sheet must be completed at case closing. (See Out-Patient procedure that follows.)

II.   Out Patients

    Definition of Out Patients

    Out Patients are all situations seen for social work intervention when no member of the patient/core group is occupying a hospital bed.

    Out Patient applies to patients registered in the clinic and/or patient and family members seen on an ambulatory basis after in-hospital care has been completed.

A.   Out Patient Screening

    Each opened case will receive credit for screening. A method has not been developed to count screening when the case is not opened in the department except Obstetrics.

    Obstetrics screenings will be counted through the use of the current screening mechanisms which are:

MANUAL OF POLICIES AND PROCEDURES
SOCIAL SERVICE DEPARTMENT

EXHIBIT 7 (continued)

SUBJECT: REPORTING FOR THE SYSTEM FOR HOSPITAL UNIFORM REPORTING (SHUR)

Index Under	File #	Date
Operating Functions, Policies and Procedures	Section 2 Item 2-9	Issued 12/78

      1.   Patient Questionnaires

      2.   Social Worker/Nurse Team and report results to the receptionist.

B.   <u>Out Patient Assessments</u>

      Each opened case will be credited for assessment.

C.   <u>Out Patient Problem Focused Intervention</u>

      Relative Value Units are assigned for each session as reported on the daily activity sheet multiplied by the number of problems addressed in that session. (See schedule attached). The staff member will, whenever recording a direct service on the registration form and/or the daily transaction sheet, put the number of problems addressed in the last column at the right-hand side of the page.

      At the time of closing, the completed problem classification sheet should be attached to the statistical closing sheet.

<u>Recapitulation of Practice Staff Member's Responsibility</u>

<u>Note</u>:   Most of the data on screenings, assessments, and interventions will be picked up by Statistical Staff. Each social worker will:

      1.   Complete the Problem Classification Sheet at time of patient's discharge from the hospital.

      2.   Complete the Problem Classification Sheet on each case at closing.

      3.   Stipulate the number of problems addressed at each session with an out-patient (as defined above) in the last column of the daily activity sheet.

MANUAL OF POLICIES AND PROCEDURES
SOCIAL SERVICE DEPARTMENT

EXHIBIT 7 (continued)

SUBJECT: REPORTING FOR THE SYSTEM FOR HOSPITAL UNIFORM REPORTING (SHUR)

(page 6 of 6 pages)

Index Under	File #	Date
Operating Functions, Policies and Procedures	Section 2 Item 2-9	Issued 12/78

<u>Recording</u>

It is essential that the Medical Chart recording conform with the information reported. All case records must reflect:

a. assessment

b. problems worked with during hospitalization

c. each out-patient visit must be recorded with problems addressed stated

d. closing must reflect problems addressed and outcome

e. accuracy is essential

MANUAL OF POLICIES AND PROCEDURES
SOCIAL SERVICE DEPARTMENT

EXHIBIT 7 (continued)

Patient Name _____   Worker Name _____

Unit Number _____   Worker Number _____

Check one:
    Inpatient discharge Case _____
    Ambulatory Closing   _____
                                        (do not complete: for office use)
    If Inpatient: Length of Stay _____ days
        Date of Admission _____
        Date of Discharge _____

Psycho Social Problems

Instructions: Circle the number of each Psycho-Social Problem dealt with. Then for each circled Problem circle one and only one letter in PART I (A-D) and circle one and only one letter in PART II (E-J). If a particular case does not fit into the outcome categories, use the other side of this form and describe the outcome. Turn this form in with each Discharge from Inpatient Service; and at Closing from Ambulatory Service.

Problem	I — Problem Status				II — Outside Resource Referral Status					
	Resolved	Improved	Situation Unchanged	Situation Worsened	Resource Not Needed	Adequate Resource Obtained	Inadequate Resource Obtained	No Resource Available	Patient and/or Family Refuses Resources	Resource no Longer Needed-Patient Died
A. Patient Functioning										
1. Coping with interpersonal relationships (e.g., marital problems; communication problems; sibling rivalry; behavior in school; care of children; role boundaries confused).	A	B	C	D	E	F	G	H	I	J
2. Family interrelationships adversely affect patient's condition and/or response to hospital.	A	B	C	D	E	F	G	H	I	J
3. Patient has problems in self-esteem; feelings of inadequacy; or in sexual functioning.	A	B	C	D	E	F	G	H	I	J
4. Patient anxiety stress or depressive reactions related to diagnosis, medical procedures, prognosis or treatment, dying, etc.	A	B	C	D	E	F	G	H	I	J
5. Patient reactions cause problems for staff (e.g., acting-out behavior, AMA discharge, etc.)	A	B	C	D	E	F	G	H	I	J
6. Patient having problems as a result of illness/disorder/pregnancy - patient role problems.	A	B	C	D	E	F	G	H	I	J
7. Patient anxiety stress or depression (eg, chronic)	A	B	C	D	E	F	G	H	I	J
8. Financial management (e.g., patient has problems managing own resources).	A	B	C	D	E	F	G	H	I	J
9. Educational and vocational functioning problems.	A	B	C	D	E	F	G	H	I	J
10. Health education needed (e.g., family planning and infant care classes).	A	B	C	D	E	F	G	H	I	J
B. Family Functioning with Relation to Patient Illness										
11. Family members need help in coping with patient's needs.	A	B	C	D	E	F	G	H	I	J
12. Coping with grief and bereavement.	A	B	C	D	E	F	G	H	I	J
13. Family interrelationships adversely affect patient's condition and/or response to hospital.	A	B	C	D	E	F	G	H	I	J
14. Family having problems as result of illness/disorder/pregnancy-patient/family role problems.	A	B	C	D	E	F	G	H	I	J
15. Family reactions cause problems for staff (e.g., acting-out behavior, AMA discharge, etc.)	A	B	C	D	E	F	G	H	I	J
16. Family anxiety stress or depressive reactions related to diagnosis, medical procedures, prognosis or treatment, dying, etc.	A	B	C	D	E	F	G	H	I	J

11/22/78   (OVER)

EXHIBIT 7 (continued)

Page 2

	I Problem Status				II Outside Resource Referral Status					
	Resolved	Improved	Situation Unchanged	Situation Worsened	Resource Not Needed	Adequate Resource Obtained	Inadequate Resource Obtained	No Resource Available	Patient and/or Family Refuses Resources	Resource no Longer Needed-Patient Died

Psycho Social Problems (continued)

	A	B	C	D	E	F	G	H	I	J
17. Family anxiety stress or depression (e.g., chronic)	A	B	C	D	E	F	G	H	I	J
18. Financial management (e.g., family has problems managing own resources).	A	B	C	D	E	F	G	H	I	J
19. Health education needed (e.g., family planning & infant care classes)										
C. Environmental Needs										
20. Financial assistance (e.g., application for SSD)	A	B	C	D	E	F	G	H	I	J
21. Housing unsuitable for continuing needs (eg, too many stairs, inadequate kitchen, security).	A	B	C	D	E	F	G	H	I	J
22. Transportation services needed.	A	B	C	D	E	F	G	H	I	J
D. Home Care Service Needs (with respect to outpatient or discharge planning for inpatient)										
23. Home and health supports needed (coordinated home care program).	A	B	C	D	E	F	G	H	I	J
24. Home supports needed (e.g., homemaker, home health aide, babysitter, day care.)	A	B	C	D	E	F	G	H	I	J
25. Concrete aids medically recommended (telephone, appliances, prosthesis, equipment, etc.)	A	B	C	D	E	F	G	H	I	J
E. Temporary Care Needs (with respect to outpatient or discharge planning for inpatient)										
26. Temporary institutional care away from home.	A	B	C	D	E	F	G	H	I	J
27. Temporary care of dependent child (or children) during patient's hospitalization.	A	B	C	D	E	F	G	H	I	J
28. Temporary housing (eg, as necessary pending treatment out of patient's own community).	A	B	C	D	E	F	G	H	I	J
F. Long Term Care Needs (with respect to outpatient or discharge planning for inpatients)										
29. Permanent placement required for child (or children) (eg, adoption, foster home).	A	B	C	D	E	F	G	H	I	J
30. Sheltered care needed (eg, halfway house; foster home for adults).	A	B	C	D	E	F	G	H	I	J
31. Long term institutional care needed.	A	B	C	D	E	F	G	H	I	J
G. Community Support Needs										
32. Long term ambulatory care needed (e.g., psychiatric OPD services; other social agencies; day hospital).	A	B	C	D	E	F	G	H	I	J
33. Letters or reports needed for other agencies.	A	B	C	D	E	F	G	H	I	J
34. Legal services needed	A	B	C	D	E	F	G	H	I	J
35. Visiting nurse services needed	A	B	C	D	E	F	G	H	I	J
36. Social agency needed	A	B	C	D	E	F	G	H	I	J
H. Hospital Services										
37. Hospital service complaints	A	B	C	D	E	F	G	H	I	J
38. Coordinating hospital services	A	B	C	D		F	G	H	I	J
I. Other	A	B	C	D		F	G	H	I	J

Total Number of Problems Dealt With _____

EXHIBIT 8

Problem/Outcome Validity Study

Form A
4/1/78

Case # ☐ ☐ ☐ ☐ ☐
1 2 3 4 5

Pt. Service ☐
6

Pt. Sex ☐
(M, F) 6

Pt. Age ☐ ☐
(01-99) 7 8

Pt. Status ☐
A=Alive
B=Deceased 9

A=Medical (include
 10 sub-specialties)
B=Obstetrics/Gynecology
C=Pediatrics
D=Psychiatry
E=Surgery (include
 sub-specialties)
F=Other _____ (specify)

Education of Social Worker(s) ☐ ☐
11 12

Use one letter (A-I) for each worker.
Primary Worker in Box #11; If no second
worker leave Box #12 blank. A=PhD or DSW
in Social Work; B=MSW; C=MA or PhD in
other field; D=BSW; E=BA or BS; F=AA or AS;
G=RN; H=High School; I=Other (Specify)

Instructions: Circle the number of each Psycho-
Social Problem of Primary Client (limit is 3)
with which you dealt. Then for each circled
Problem circle one and only one letter in
PART I (A-D) and circle one and only one letter
in Part II (E-J). Turn this form in with each
closing during the month of May.

PROBLEMS DEALT WITH

	OUTCOME									
	I Problem Status				II Outside Resource Referral Status					
PROBLEMS DEALT WITH	Resolved	Improved (but not resolved)	Situation Unchanged	Situation Worsened	Resource Not Needed	Adequate Resource Obtained	Inadequate Resource Obtained	No Resource Available	Patient and/or Family Refuses	Resource no Longer Needed-Patient Died
13. Concrete aids medically recommended (telephone, appliances, prosthesis, equipment, etc).	A	B	C	D	E	F	G	H	I	J
14. Coping with grief reaction and bereavement.	A	B	C	D	E	F	G	H	I	J
15. Coping with interpersonal relations (eg. marital problems; school problems; care of children)	A	B	C	D	E	F	G	H	I	J
16. Educational or vocational functioning problems.	A	B	C	D	E	F	G	H	I	J
17. Family interrelationships adversely affect patient's condition and/or response to hospital.	A	B	C	D	E	F	G	H	I	J
18. Family members need help in coping with patient's needs.	A	B	C	D	E	F	G	H	I	J
19. Financial management/assistance/applications	A	B	C	D	E	F	G	H	I	J
20. Health Education Needed (eg. Family Planning)	A	B	C	D	E	F	G	H	I	J

	A	B	C	D	E	F	G	H	I	J
21. Home health supports needed (coordinated home care program).	A	B	C	D	E	F	G	H	I	J
22. Home supports needed (eg: homemaker, home health aid, baby-sitter, day care).	A	B	C	D	E	F	G	H	I	J
23. Hospital Service Complaints.	A	B	C	D	E	F	G	H	I	J
24. Housing unsuitable for continuing needs (eg: too many stairs, inadequate kitchen, security).	A	B	C	D	E	F	G	H	I	J
25. Legal services needed.	A	B	C	D	E	F	G	H	I	J
26. Letters or Reports Needed for Other Agencies	A	B	C	D	E	F	G	H	I	J
27. Long term ambulatory care needed (eg. psychiatric OPD services; other social agencies; day hospital).	A	B	C	D	E	F	G	H	I	J
28. Long term institutional care needed.	A	B	C	D	E	F	G	H	I	J
29. Patient/family having role disorder problems as result of illness/disorder/pregnancy	A	B	C	D	E	F	G	M	I	J
30. Patient/family problems with staff	A	B	C	D	E	F	G	H	I	J
31. Patient/family anxiety stress or depressive reactions related to diagnosis, medical procedures, prognosis or treatment, dying, etc.	A	B	C	D	E	F	G	H	I	J
32. Patient/family anxiety stress or depression (eg. thought and mood disturbance; psychomatization)	A	B	C	D	E	F	G	H	I	J
33. Patient has problems in self-esteem; feelings of inadequacy; or in sexual functioning.	A	B	C	D	E	F	G	H	I	J
34. Permanent Placement required for child(ren) (eg. adoption, foster home)	A	B	C	D	E	F	G	H	I	J
35. Psycho-social evaluation only for assessment of ability to use treatment, or re. admission to hospital.	A	B	C	D	E	F	G	H	I	J
36. Sheltered care needed (eg. halfway house; foster home for adults).	A	B	C	D	E	F	G	M	I	J
37. Social isolation/withdrawal	A	B	C	D	E	F	G	H	I	J
38. Temporary care of dependent child(ren) during patient's hospitalization.	A	B	C	D	E	F	G	H	I	J
39. Temporary institutional care away from home.	A	B	C	D	E	F	G	H	I	J
40. Transportation services needed.	A	B	C	D	E	F	G	H	I	J
41. Visiting nurses service needed.	A	B	C	D	E	F	G	H	I	J
42. Other (write in) _____	A	B	C	D	E	F	G	H	I	J

EXHIBIT 9

Form C

"Primary Client" Follow-up Telephone Interview

Name: _____

Address: _____

Telephone: _____

Check One:
    Call Completed _____
    Can't Find _____
    Refusal_____
    Deferred _____

Relationship to patient (If primary client is the patient, note this)_____

Is patient deceased? Yes ☐ No ☐

HELLO, _____? I AM MRS. _____ FROM THE RESEARCH DIVISION OF THE SOCIAL SERVICE DEPARTMENT OF MOUNT SINAI HOSPITAL. WE ARE INTERESTED IN IMPROVING THE DELIVERY OF SOCIAL SERVICES IN THE HOSPITAL AND WE WOULD VERY MUCH APPRECIATE YOUR ANSWERS TO A FEW QUESTIONS. LET ME ASSURE YOU YOUR ANSWERS WILL BE COMPLETELY CONFIDENTIAL. IT WILL ONLY TAKE A FEW MINUTES OF YOUR TIME.

---

1. How did you find out there was a social worker at Mount Sinai?
   (In other words, did anyone refer you to or tell you about the social worker?)
   If yes, who? _____
   If yes, what did they tell you the social worker would be able to do for you?
   _____

   _____

2. How often did you see the social worker? Frequently _____?
   Sometimes _____? Rarely _____?

3. Would you have liked to have seen the social worker: More often _____?
   The same _____? Less often _____? If answer is not "Same" probe for why?

   _____

   _____

4. Did the social worker seem to understand what you wanted? Yes ( ) No ( ) Unsure ( )

5. What in particular did you and the social worker work on?

   _____

   _____

6. Was she able to help you? Yes ( ) No ( ) Unsure ( )

EXHIBIT 9 (continued)

Case # _____

-2-

7. I am now going to read you some ways in which hospital social workers can help people. Did the social worker at Mount Sinai help you in any of these ways? (Interviewer, read each item separately)

    A. Help you or your family to become less worried or tense Yes ( ) No ( )

    B. Offered advice Yes ( )   No ( )

    C. Helped you get more information from the doctor Yes ( )   No ( )

    D. Helped you get a particular service (such as visiting nurse, convalescent home or financial help) Yes ( )   No ( )

    E. Talked about many problems Yes ( )   No ( )

    F. Referred you to another agency Yes ( )   No ( )

8. Were you satisfied with the services received? Yes ( )   No ( )

Why? _____

_____

9. Do you think seeing the social worker earlier than you did would have been more help?

    Yes ( ) No ( )

If NO, ask why not?

_____

_____

If YES, would you have preferred seeing her:

    _____a) Before starting contact with the hospital
    _____b) During the first few days of contact with the hospital
    _____c) Other - write out _____

                      _____

                      _____

10. If any of your friends or members of your family had a problem, would you advise them to see a social worker? Yes ( ) No ( ) Unsure ( )

If NO, why not? _____

_____

If UNSURE, why? _____

_____

EXHIBIT 9 (continued)

-3-

11. Is there any way you feel that the social workers at Mount Sinai could improve
their services? _____

_____

_____

_____

_____

_____

_____

Thank you. This completes the interview. Do you have any questions or comments?

_____

_____

_____

_____

Interviewer Notes (after interview)

_____

_____

_____

_____

_____

_____

_____

_____

_____

_____

EXHIBIT 10

Social Work Services

Social work services shall be readily available to the patient, Principle
the patient's family, and other persons significant to the pa-
tient, in order to facilitate adjustment of these individuals to the
impact of illness, and to promote maximum benefits from the
health care services provided.

Social work services shall be well organized, properly directed, Standard I
staffed with a sufficient number of qualified individuals, and ap-
propriately integrated with other units and departments/services
of the hospital.

The relationship of social work services to other units and departments/ INTERPRETATION
services of the hospital shall be specified within the overall hospital organizational plan. The provision of social work services shall be based on individual patient need and the availability of community resources. Collaboration with representatives of the hospital administration, medical staff,
nursing service, other services involved in direct patient care, and, as appro- 15
priate, representatives of community organizations shall be assured in the
development and implementation of the social work department/service
program.
  Social work services may be provided through various methods, depending upon the scope of services offered by the hospital and the resources 20
available in the community. In order of preference, social work services
may be provided through:

• an organized social work department/service within the hospital that
  has a qualified social work department/service director on a full-time
  basis. 25

EXHIBIT 10 (continued)

- a qualified social worker employed on a part-time basis.
- outside social work services that are obtained through a written agreement with another hospital, school of social work, community agency or health department, or another qualified organization providing such consultation services. Agreements for such outside services should define the role and responsibility of the hospital and the outside service.

5

When a hospital does not have a full-time or part-time qualified social worker, it must have a designated employee to coordinate and assure the provision of social work services. The employee must be knowledgeable about pertinent community agencies, institutions, and other resources. Whenever possible, this individual should be the equivalent of a social work assistant.

10

When a qualified social worker is not available on at least a regular part-time basis to direct and provide social work services, a qualified social worker shall provide consultation. The regular visits, services performed, findings, and recommendations of such an individual shall be documented in writing. The frequency of visits shall assure that at least the requirements of this section of the *Manual* are met.

15

Regardless of the mechanism used to provide social work services, facilities should be readily accessible, and should permit privacy for interviews and counseling, as needed.

20

In a hospital with an organized social work department/service, a qualified social worker shall direct the provision of social work services. This individual shall be responsible to the chief executive officer or his administrative or medical designee. The social work department/service director shall have the authority and responsibility for carrying out established policies, and for providing overall direction in the continuing operation of the service. The director shall assure that a review of the quality and appropriateness of social work services is performed and that action, as needed, is taken based on the findings of the review activities. Social work services shall be provided by a sufficient number of qualified personnel. Such personnel may include social work supervisors; graduate social workers, such as research social workers, caseworkers, and group workers; social work assistants; and other supportive personnel.

25

30

The size of the staff should be related to the scope and complexity of the hospital's services and the social needs of the patients served. When emergency, rehabilitative, psychiatric, long-term or home care services are provided by the hospital, related social work services are a valuable adjunct to good care. Reference is made to the Rehabilitation Programs/Services and Home Care Services sections of this *Manual*.

35

40

Social work department/service personnel shall be currently licensed, registered, or certified, as legally required.

Standard II   **Social work service personnel shall be prepared for their responsibilities in the provision of social work services through appropriate training and education programs.**

INTERPRETATION   The education, training, and experience of personnel who provide social work services shall be documented, and shall be related to each individual's level of participation in the provision of social work services. This may require a formal education/training program as a prerequisite, or on-the-

EXHIBIT 10 (continued)

job training. New personnel shall receive an orientation of sufficient duration and substance to prepare them for their role in the provision of hospital
social work services. As appropriate, individuals providing social work
services shall receive instruction in:

- recognition of and attention to the psychosocial needs of patients and   5
  their families.
- evaluation and treatment of crisis situations and disability resulting
  from the emotional, social, and economic stresses of illness.
- assisting the medical, nursing, and other health care personnel in ar-
  ranging for prescribed medical (including psychiatric) alternative   10
  treatment; and participating in discharge planning functions. To facilitate continuity of care, assistance should be provided to the patient
  and the patient's family in adapting to the patient care plan, whether
  the service provided is to be continued in a home care or out-of-home
  care setting.   15
- patient safety and infection control.

Personnel providing social work services shall participate in relevant continuing education, including in-service programs. The director of the social
work department/service or qualified designees should contribute to the
in-service education of social work and other health care personnel. Educa-   20
tion programs for social work department/service personnel shall be based,
at least in part, on the results of social work department/service evaluation
studies. Outside educational opportunities shall be provided whenever feasible, at least for supervisory social work service personnel. The extent of
participation in continuing education shall be documented, and shall be   25
realistically related to the size of the staff and to the scope and complexity
of the social work services provided.

Social work services shall be guided by written policies and pro-   Standard III
cedures.

There shall be written policies and procedures concerning the scope and   INTERPRETATION
conduct of social work services. The director of the social work department/
service is responsible for assuring that the development and implementation
of the policies and procedures are carried out in collaboration with other
appropriate clinical and administrative representatives. Such policies and
procedures should be subjected to timely review, revised as necessary, dated   35
to indicate the time of the last review, and enforced. Social work depart-
ment/service policies and procedures shall be consistent with hospital and
medical staff rules and regulations relating to patient care and medical
records, and with legal requirements. The policies and procedures shall
relate to at least the following: 40

- Type of services available;
- Identification of patients and their families requiring social work
  services;
- Confidentiality of information;
- Consultation and referral procedures;   45
- Relationship of other hospital services and outside agencies;
- Maintenance of required records, statistical information, and reports;

EXHIBIT 10 (continued)

- Home environmental evaluations for attending practitioners, as requested;
- The role of the social work department/service in discharge planning; and
5 - Social work functions resulting from federal, state, and local requirements.

Standard IV **Adequate documentation of social work services provided shall be included in the patient's medical record.**

INTERPRETATION When social work services are provided to a patient, clear and concise
10 entries shall be made in the patient's medical record to permit regular communication with physicians, nurses, and other personnel involved in the patient's care. As appropriate, pertinent information relating to the following should be included:

15 - Observations and social assessment of the patient and, as relevant, of the patient's family;
- Proposed plan for providing any required social work services;
- Any social therapy/rehabilitation provided to the patient and the patient's family;
- Social work summaries, including any recommendations for follow-up.

20 As appropriate, other pertinent information should also be included in the medical record such as home environment evaluations for the attending practitioner, cooperative activities with community agencies, and follow-up reports.

Reference is also made to the Medical Record Services section of this
25 *Manual.*

Standard V **The quality and appropriateness of social work services provided to patients shall be regularly reviewed, evaluated, and assured through the establishment of quality control mechanisms.**

INTERPRETATION The director of social work services shall be responsible for assuring that
30 a review of the appropriateness and effectiveness of social work services is accomplished in a timely manner, including services provided to inpatients and, where applicable, to outpatients, emergency patients, and patients in a hospital-administered home care program. The review should be performed at least twice each year, and shall involve the use of the medical
35 record and preestablished criteria. Such criteria shall relate at least to the indications for providing social work services and to the effectiveness of required social work interventions. The review of social work services may be performed as part of any overall hospital patient care evaluation program. Particular attention shall be given to the appropriateness and effec-
40 tiveness of the transfer of patients to long-term care facilities and to home placement with supportive services, and to crisis intervention in the emergency services. The quality and appropriateness of social work services provided in the hospital by outside sources shall be included in the review on the same regular basis. Reviews relating to the quality and appropriate-
45 ness of social work services shall be documented.

192

EXHIBIT 11

SUBJECT: <u>RECORDING EXPECTATIONS</u>

<u>Policy</u>

A current record of Social Service activity is to be entered into the medical chart on behalf of each patient. It is expected that this recording will improve patient care by promoting communication of the social service contribution. This will also serve the administrative purpose of accountability for the department's activity.

Chart notations can be done in varied form: pink stickers, handwritten notes with preference in some areas for red ink, special forms such as the one currently being utilized in the Pregnancy Interruption Service in Obstetrics.

The policy does not define recording to be done on cases used for learning purposes. The type of recording in these instances will be determined by the supervisor and worker in accordance with the learning areas they have defined. Recording for demonstration, teaching, and research will also be defined in accordance with the individual need.

I. <u>Recording Expectations</u>

    A. <u>Frequency of Recording</u>

        1. Requirements for individual Social Service contacts, both inpatient and outpatient.

           a) Opening statement: there must be an initial statement in every medical chart at the time of opening in Social Service. This may be either legibly handwritten, by typed sticker, or by special form.
           b) Progress notes must be added as follows:
               (1) Inpatients: must be once a week (or more frequently at worker's discretion) and number of interviews noted.
               (2) Outpatients: for once weekly or more contact, progress notes must be done weekly. For contacts less than once a week, notations must be made after each contact.
               (3) Admission note: for patients currently active to Social Service.

           c) Transfer of case to another worker should be noted in medical chart.
           d) Discharge note: must be made in all inpatient medical charts on occasion of patient's discharge whether or not case to remain active in Social Service.
           e) Closing statement must be entered in all medical charts at point of cessation of contact.

        2. <u>Requirements for group contacts</u>

           a) Ongoing groups: entries will be made in medical charts of each patient once every four weeks (or more often at worker's discretion).

EXHIBIT 11 (continued)

b) For groups that meet on a one time basis: indication of attendance will be noted in medical chart. For outpatient groups these notations will be done by clerical staff from registration forms. On inpatient groups notation in medical chart must be made by worker.

3. Since all recording will be current and available through the medical charts, there will be no need to do vacation dictation. It is an expectation that workers will fully inform covering worker of current status of caseload prior to leaving on vacation.

B. Guidelines for Content

1. Opening statement should include:

a) Reason for referral and by whom referred.
b) Social assessment (family setup, influential persons, worker's impressions regarding patient and family, including strength as well as problems).
c) Attitudes around illness and treatment.
d) Social Service focus and plan of action.
e) Recommendations for handling including patient/family ability to comprehend.

Consideration must be given regarding what to leave out, such as unverified factual data, comments on medical treatment, or information that does not have bearing for other disciplines, i.e., marital infidelity.

2. Progress notes: must be brief, concise, and focused on Social Service activity and on any changes in assessment or planning.

3. Admission note: should summarize information pertinent to current hospitalization.

4. Discharge note: to include worker's ongoing plan.

5. Closing note: should include the initial problem(s), how each handled, additional matters that came up during contact, and how handled, and reason(s), for closing out contact.

II. Mechanisms for Recording - both individual and group contacts
Note: The standards of the Joint Commission on Accreditation of Hospitals require that all entries be signed.

A. Inpatient

1. Either handwritten directly into medical chart or written on Form #M-2, to be done as a typed sticker worker places in medical chart.

B. Outpatient

1. Handwritten notations if medical chart available at time of patient contact. Duplicate copies for Social Service can be made by worker at her discretion.

EXHIBIT 11 (continued)

2. Sticker to be typed, returned for signature and then placed into medical chart by the clerical staff.

3. Form to be used for writing up outpatient progress notes.
   a. Progress notes to be written as noted in "Frequency of Recording" above. These must be done on Form #M-2 and sent for secretarial typing.

C. Duplicate copy of sticker will be placed in Social Service records filed in secretarial pool area. Workers will keep the yellow registration form and notes in a notebook for their own, and covering worker's use, in place of the Social Service record.

D. Pertinent summaries, forms or correspondence will be kept by the worker while the case is active (folder to be provided). At closing, this material will be sent to the secretarial pool for filing.

E. Chart entries, whether written or typed, should be in a uniform format (example attached).

F. Each worker should do a daily self-check by making a check mark in the extreme right hand margin of the daily statistical sheet for each interview for which she has made a chart notation.

Revised 11/6/72

The Mount Sinai Hospital
Department of Social Work Services

EXHIBIT 12

Chart Notation Review

Name of Patient: _____   Worker: _____

Service or Clinic: _____   Name of Reviewer: _____

Unit Number: _____   Date Case Reviewed: _____

Number of chart notes reviewed _____ opening _____ progress _____

1) Date case opened _____   Date of opening note _____
   Dates of progress notes _____
   Date of closing note, if any _____

2) Does frequency reflect the established policy?   Yes _____   No _____
   (comments) _____

   _____

3) Is the reason for referral and by whom clear?   Yes _____   No _____
   (comments) _____

   _____

4) Is the social assessment of patient clear?   Yes _____   No _____
   (comments) _____

   _____

   _____

5) Are problems clearly defined?   Yes _____   No _____   (comments) _____

   _____

6) Are goals clearly stated? Yes _____   No _____   (comments) _____

   _____

7) Is the description of interventions clear? Yes _____   No _____
   (comments) _____

   _____

8) General impression: Please explain _____

   _____

   _____

   _____

7/18/75 - M-14

EXHIBIT 13

THE MOUNT SINAI HOSPITAL
DEPARTMENT OF SOCIAL WORK SERVICES

Guidelines For Content of Chart Notes

1. The initial entry should include date, source of referral or reason for social worker's initial contact with patient/family. (Marginal date will be accepted as date of initial contact unless otherwise indicated.)

2. Each chart should include an assessment stating some factual data relevant to the patient's medical condition and psycho-social situation.

3. The workers' impressions should reflect a clear diagnostic appraisal of the patient/family as related to the medical problem and social functioning ability.

4. Problems identified should be clearly stated.

5. All information should be relevant to the problem(s) identified.

6. If worker is unable to make a full assessment at time of initial contact(s) this should be documented with reasons.

7. Collaborative contacts with other disciplines should be indicated as they relate to social workers' assessment, diagnostic appraisal and plans for intervention.

8. Contract should be mutually agreed upon by worker and patient/family. This should be clearly stated. If not, worker should document reasons.

9. The contract and goals should be arrived at via the assessment and indicate relationship given to those problems of primary concern to patient/family.

10. Contract should be established in interest of or on behalf of patient with priorities given to those problems of primary concern to patient/family.

11. Problems identified for social work intervention should be clearly stated. Those problems not to be dealt with should be acknowledged with statement as to why.

12. The treatment plan should be appropriate to the problem(s) identified and stated in such a way that it can be implemented by another social worker (staff member) handling the case.

13. Interventions should reflect adequate involvement with other disciplines as well as family members or significant others.

14. Progress notes should reflect worker's activity to date. Where relevant they should include ongoing assessments, changes in contract, goals and/or treatment plans.

15. Progress notes should be useful to other disciplines involved in the patient's care.

16. Disposition should include what was achieved or outcome, plan for follow-up, if any. If none, reasons should be documented.

7/76

EXHIBIT 14

MOUNT SINAI HOSPITAL
DEPARTMENT OF SOCIAL WORK SERVICES

Peer Review

TO: _____, Social Worker

FROM: Peer Review Committee

DATE: _____

YOUR PATIENT RECORD, _____, WAS SELECTED
FOR PEER REVIEW.

THE RECORD WAS REVIEWED ON _____.
                                    (date)

THE RECORD HAD _____ SOCIAL SERVICE CHART NOTATIONS.

I. ITS JUDGMENT AS TO THE QUALITY OF SOCIAL SERVICE SERVICE IS SUMMARIZED
   BELOW:

	Excellent	Good	Fair	Poor
Entry				
Assessment				
Contract				
Intervention				
Collaboration				
Overall				

II. COMMENTS AND RECOMMENDATIONS

EXHIBIT 14 (continued)

SOCIAL SERVICE ENTRY

	Y	N
1. Is the date of initial contact with social work service noted?		
2. Is the reason for initial contact clear?		
3. Is the source clear (how social service became involved)?		
4. Is the opening statement adequate?		
5. Did social service enter at the appropriate time and/or point?		
6. If NO, is it clear why social service entry was not earlier?		

Patient Record _____
Social Worker _____
Date of Review _____

DRAFT TO BE REVISED

ASSESSMENT

	Y	N
1. Is there evidence of an initial assessment?		
2. Is there evidence of ongoing assessment?		
3. Is the assessment adequate in terms of the problems identified by the worker?		
4. Does the assessment reflect adequate understanding of the patient's situation/problem?		
5. Does the assessment include a) psycho, b)social and c)physical functioning of patient?		
6. Does the assessment show an understanding of the medical condition and its implications?		
7. Does the worker give his/her impression of the patient/family?		
8. Is it clear which problems will be the focus of social work intervention?		
9. Were the appropriate problems selected for intervention?		
10. Have all appropriate problems been selected for intervention?		

CONTRACT/GOALS

	Y	N
1. Is there indication that a contract (mutual agreement on goals between worker and patient/family) has been established?		
1a. If NO, is there justification for patient of family not participating in contracting?		
2. Was the contract established with the appropriate individual(s)?		
3. Is there evidence of adequate patient/family involvement in order to establish the contract?		
4. Is the contract appropriate?		
5. Is the contact adequate?		
6. Does the contract reflect patient interest/priority rather than agency interest/priority?		
7. Should there have been a treatment plan?		
7a. If YES, is there an adequate treatment plan?		
8. Where relevant, are discrepancies between the contract and treatment plan explained?		

199

EXHIBIT 14 (continued)

INTERVENTION

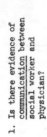

	Y	N
1. Are social work interventions identified?		
2. Are interventions noted in a way that is helpful to others?		
3. Are social work interventions consistent with the contract?		
4. Are social work interventions consistent with the treatment plan?		
5. Does intervention indicate adequate involvement of appropriate family members?		
6. Does intervention indicate adequate involvement of appropriate resources?		
7. Where relevant, does intervention take into account new developments?		
8. Are any changes in plan, goals or contract adequately explained?		
9. Is there evidence of a _good_ working relationship between worker and patient/family?		
10. Did this case receive sufficient social work attention?		
11. Was there an appropriate disposition of the case?		
11a. If NO, is a reason given?		

COLLABORATION

	Y	N
1. Is there evidence of communication between social worker and physician?		
2. Was the timing of the collaboration appropriate?		
3. Is there evidence of adequate ongoing collaboration with physician?		
3a. Was there adequate collaboration with other disciplines?		
4. Is there evidence of an effective _interdisciplinary working relationship_?		
4a. If NO, is it clear what the social worker's role and responsibility has been in attempting to establish the working relationship?		

MOUNT SINAI HOSPITAL
DEPARTMENT OF SOCIAL WORK
SERVICES

8/76

DRAFT TO BE REVISED

EXHIBIT 15

MOUNT SINAI HOSPITAL
SOCIAL SERVICE DEPARTMENT

Peer Review

TO: _____, SOCIAL WORKER

FROM: PEER REVIEW COMMITTEE   DATE: _____

YOUR PATIENT RECORD _____ WAS REVIEWED.

OUR JUDGMENT AS TO QUALITY IS SUMMARIZED BELOW:	Y	N	NA
1. Are the date and source of contact with Social Service noted?			
2. Is the reason for Social Service involvement clear?			
2a. If no, is there justification for Social Service involvement?			
3. Were appropriate actions taken?			
4. Is there evidence of appropriate interdisciplinary communication/ collaboration?			
5. Did this case receive sufficient social work attention?			
6. Was there appropriate disposition?			
6a. If no, is a reason given?			

7. What is the overall quality of Social Service?

Excellent [　]   Good [　]   Fair [　]   Poor [　]

8. Comments

12/76

201

EXHIBIT 16

Form A - PR Screening
DRAFT TO DE REVISED

MOUNT SINAI HOSPITAL
DEPARTMENT OF SOCIAL WORK SERVICES

Peer Review

TO: _____, Social Worker

FROM: _____

DATE: _____

DATE CASE CLOSED _____

YOUR PATIENT RECORD, _____, WAS SELECTED
FOR PEER REVIEW.

I. IT WAS NOT POSSIBLE TO REVIEW THIS RECORD AT THIS TIME FOR THE FOLLOWING
    REASON(S):

    a. _____ The record was unavailable at this time.

    b. _____ There were no chart notations to review.

    c. _____ The chart notes did not fall within the dates
             designated for Peer Review.

    d. _____ Opened/closed cases and charts with one note are
             not suitable for review with the current review
             forms. Therefore, additional charts will be re-
             quested for screening and review.

    e. _____ Other _____
                     _____.

II. COMMENTS AND RECOMMENDATIONS

    f. _____ No action required of social worker at this time;

    g. _____ Clarification or confirmation of situation is required
             of social worker by _____;
                          (date)

    h. _____ Clarification or confirmation of situation is being
             sought elsewhere _____;

    i. _____ Other _____
                     _____.

10/76

EXHIBIT 17
OPEN PRECEPTORSHIP

WORKER: _____

PRECEPTOR: _____

PART A:
CONTRACT: _____

_____

_____

_____

_____

PART B: PART C:
IDENTIFIED LEARNING AREAS: CONSIDERABLE   SOME PROGRESS   NO
                                     PROGRESS SHOWN SHOWN   PROGRESS
                                                                     SHOWN

ADDITIONAL COMMENTS: _____

_____

_____

_____

SIGNED:

WORKER: _____

PRECEPTOR: _____

203

EXHIBIT 18

Mount Sinai Hospital
Department of Social Work Services

CONTINUING EDUCATION PROGRAM EVALUATION FORM

Seminar number _____

Name (Optional)_____

Seminar Leader _____

In order to assess the quality of our education program we are asking you to
fill out our evaluation form. Thank you for your cooperation.

I. Please list the major purposes of the seminar you attended.

       1. _____

       2. _____

       3. _____

       4. _____

Comments: _____

_____

_____

II. Did you learn anything in the seminar?   Yes _____

                                No _____

If yes please.list the major learning content.

       1. _____

       2. _____

       3. _____

       4. _____

Comments: _____

_____

_____

_____

EXHIBIT 18 (continued)

III. Application to Practice (Check one for each category).

	Inadequate	Adequate	Good	Outstanding
A - Application to work in hospital				
B - Enhancement of skills				
C - Introduction of new ideas				

Comments: _____

_____

_____

IV. Evaluation of Instructor (Check one for each category).

	Inadequate	Adequate	Good	Outstanding
A - Knowledge				
B - Presentation				
C - Stimulation				
D - Quality of material (readings and cases, etc.)				
E - Overall rating of instructor				

Comments: _____

_____

_____

V. Evaluation of Learning Group Process (Check one for each category).

	Inadequate	Adequate	Good	Outstanding
A - Quality of members preparation for group.				
B - Quality of presentations				
C - Groups support for encouraging participation.				
D - Groups response to your presentations				
E - Groups accomplishment of learning goals.				

Comments: _____

_____

_____

205

EXHIBIT 18 (continued)

VI. Content of Seminar (Check one for each category)

	Inadequate	Adequate	Good	Outstanding
A - Social Service Entry				
B - Assessment Skills				
C - Collaborative Skills				
D - Contracting Skills				
E.- Interventive Skills				
F - Outcome Evaluation Skills				
G - Chart Notation				
H - Family Oriented Practice				
I - Group Practice				
J - Development of Service				

Comments: _____

_____

_____

EXHIBIT 19

HUNTER COLLEGE SCHOOL OF SOCIAL WORK
129 East 79th Street, New York, N.Y. 10021

Interview Recording <u>Guide</u>

The purpose of this guide is to provide direction for learning the substantive content and process of an interview.

Worker's Name:_____ Date:_____

Client's(s') Name(s)_____ Interview Number_____

1. Objectives of Interview

    What did you have in mind for work with client(s) in this interview?

    Indicate whether and how objectives were affected by inputs from other professionals.

2. Identification of Major Themes

    a. Briefly summarize what you and client(s) talked about (content).

    b. Identify client's(s) behavior in relation to content (affect, i.e., emotional tone, body language, speech patterns).

3. Detail two interactions between you and client(s) and/or other staff.

4. Interview Assessment

    a. Do you think you and client(s) had the same expectations for interview? If not, discuss differences.

    b. What do you think was accomplished in interview:

        1. toward solving the problem(s)?

        2. toward your increased understanding of person/problem situation?

    c. What are your next steps?
       Include collaborative work (if indicated)

5. What did you like and/or dislike about interview?

    What would you like to discuss?

cw

EXHIBIT 20

Criteria for Identifying the Self-Directed Worker

The following criteria may be applicable to workers on all levels; however, it is the degree and the attitude of professional self-expectation that identifies the self-directed practitioner. Implicit is a commitment toward proficiency and the ongoing, open-minded application of one's social work knowledge and skills. Whether a worker meets these criteria can be documented from practice.

1. Demonstrated ability to do critical self-evaluation of job performance, i.e., to identify areas of one's own competence as well as those of one's deficiencies.

2. Demonstrated ability to acknowledge problem areas requiring strengthening and to take responsibility for seeking and using appropriate help toward this end.

3. Ability and readiness to modify practice patterns when appropriate.

4. High degree of integration of knowledge and practice.

5. Demonstrated possession of the knowledge and skills in a range of interventive activities (e.g., individual, group, systems, and community organization).

6. Demonstrated ability to know when, the kind, and how to use and give appropriate consultation.

7. Demonstrated ability to make oneself felt planfully, i.e., that activities are governed in part by this setting and health care system in general. Demonstrated ability to be a change agent directly—with a disciplined approach—seizing opportunities as presented with conscious awareness and a careful assessment of other personnel and the consequences to the Department.

8. Demonstrated assumption of responsibility in assessing and contributing toward, or initiating a service program, i.e., a high degree of innovative skills, and then having the ability selectively to use appropriate supervision in implementing such.

9. Assumption of teaching responsibilities in relation to other hospital personnel, and the School of Medicine.

10. Participation in and leadership of special committees within the Department, the Hospital, and the community.

11. Demonstrated skill in effective collaborative practice and reciprocal sharing of work within this setting as well as with others outside of the Hospital.

12. Demonstration of professional concern and sense of responsibility regarding expenditures in the delivery of services, i.e., recognition of the relatedness of administrative responsibilities to delivery of service. Have the professional maturity to understand the organization and delivery of services.

13. Demonstrated interest in continuing education. Have a basic definition of what one needs for one's own development and be responsible for and involved in pushing for one's continuing education.

About the Authors

CHAUNCEY A. ALEXANDER, ACSW, CSW
Executive Director
National Association of Social Workers
Washington, D.C.

BARBARA BERKMAN, D.S.W.
Adjunct Associate Professor of Community Medicine
Mount Sinai School of Medicine
City University of New York

PHYLLIS CAROFF, D.S.W.
Professor
Hunter College School of Social Work
City University of New York

ROSLYN CHERNESKY, D.S.W.
Associate Professor
Columbia University School of Social Work
New York, N.Y.

HANNAH LIPSKY, M.S.
Assistant Director
Department of Social Work Services
The Mount Sinai Hospital
Instructor in Community Medicine
Mount Sinai School of Medicine
City University of New York

JANICE PANETH, M.S.
Associate Director
Department of Social Work Services
The Mount Sinai Hospital
Assistant Professor of Community Medicine
Mount Sinai School of Medicine
City University of New York

JANE PARSONS, M.S.W.
Social Worker
Department of Social Work Services
The Mount Sinai Hospital
New York, N.Y.

HELEN REHR, D.S.W.
Director
Department of Social Work Services
The Mount Sinai Hospital
Edith J. Baerwald Professor of Community Medicine (Social Work)
Mount Sinai School of Medicine
City University of New York

GARY ROSENBERG, Ph.D.
Deputy Director
Department of Social Work Services
The Mount Sinai Hospital
Assistant Professor of Community Medicine
Mount Sinai School of Medicine
City University of New York

ELLEN SMITH, M.S.W.
Preceptor
Department of Social Work Services
The Mount Sinai Hospital
New York, N.Y.

DOROTHY TOPPER, M.S.W.
Social Worker
Department of Social Work Services
The Mount Sinai Hospital
New York, N.Y.

MARILYN WILSON, M.S.W.
Grant Associate
Hunter College School of Social Work
Instructor in Community Medicine
Mount Sinai School of Medicine
City University of New York

ALMA T. YOUNG, M.S.W.
Assistant Director
Department of Social Work Services
The Mount Sinai Hospital
Instructor in Community Medicine
Mount Sinai School of Medicine
City University of New York

JOAN ZOFNASS, M.S.W.
Social Worker
Department of Social Work Services
The Mount Sinai Hospital
New York, N.Y.